FIRESTARTER

FIRESTARTER

The Fiery Life & Controversial
Death of John Stallon
The Shelford Arsonist

GALILEO PUBLISHERS,
CAMBRIDGE

First published 2025 by Galileo Publishers
www.galileopublishing.co.uk

ISBN 978-1-917543-00-2

Map by www.richardbowring.co.uk
cover image © 2025 Shutterstock

EU Authorised Representative: Easy Access System Europe -
Mustamäe tee 50, 10621 Tallinn, Estonia,
gpsr.requests@easproject.com

Printed in Poland

for Brian & Jane

CONTENTS

PROLOGUE

When John Stallon passed from this earth on the seventh day of December 1833, his execution did not, in the view of many onlookers, go well.

People complained the criminal's arms were not properly bound. Mr Orridge the Governor of the County Gaol at Cambridge – whose voice rings out from newspaper reports of the hanging – insisted this was not true. The executioner, William Calcraft, checked the strapping in his usual, thorough-going way. Calcraft's fee for a hanging in the provinces was ten pounds; he was paid to leave nothing to chance.[1]

The band was threaded tight, the prisoner's arms clamped hard at the elbow.

Next, they say Stallon struggled pathetically at the end of his rope – there was kicking and jerking for some minutes. They do not mention that on the day in question, the Castle Mound at Cambridge was subject to shuddering winds. This, the newspapers say, accounts for what people saw, or thought they saw, playing out against the sky on that overcast and windswept day.

The truth is, John Stallon met his end as many of us might; breached by fear. On the short walk from the prison gate to the gallows at Castle Hill, John stumbled, not because he tripped, his toe catching in the shale or turf, but because his legs buckled beneath him. He had, at that moment, lost the power to command any part of himself.

The crowd, seeing the condemned man falter, quietened.

Gone was the diversion most expected when they stepped out from home that Saturday morning, full of holiday spirit. They came for a foretaste of the summer fairs. What they got was something more prosaic, brutal, and sad.

Mr Orridge, the Governor, stepped close and pulled Stallon to his feet. The full weight of John's despair pressed against him; a body abandoned by the terrible loosing of the mind.

During his many years as prison governor Robert Orridge had supervised the hanging of plenty of wretched souls like John Stallon. Despite the inconvenience to himself, experience taught him it went best for the 'culprit' when the mind was no longer fully present at the moment of extinction. First the mind, then the soul, swiftly evacuated. What was lowered from the rope that day would be flesh. Orridge would merely bring forward the release of the soul to Final Judgement; God's mercy – or otherwise – nudged into play by His earthly representative.

Stallon's crime? He was an incendiary – a Firestarter. His reign of terror in South Cambridgeshire lasted over four years – until he was finally accused, charged, found guilty, and sentenced.

The details of this case are a puzzle – the story does not quite add up. On the one hand, Stallon-as-arsonist was a genius; for a long time he outwitted the top detectives in the country. On the other hand, it was a project doomed from the beginning. What could possibly have been his motive? Patch together the details of John Stallon's life and you find that despite the poverty in which he and his family lived, he had much to lose. What's more, he spent his whole life in one small village, yet come the trial, he proved utterly friendless. What could explain his neighbours' coldness towards one of their own?

Almost two hundred years later, I set out to find some answers. The search begins with John Stallon, inconveniently setting the world on fire.

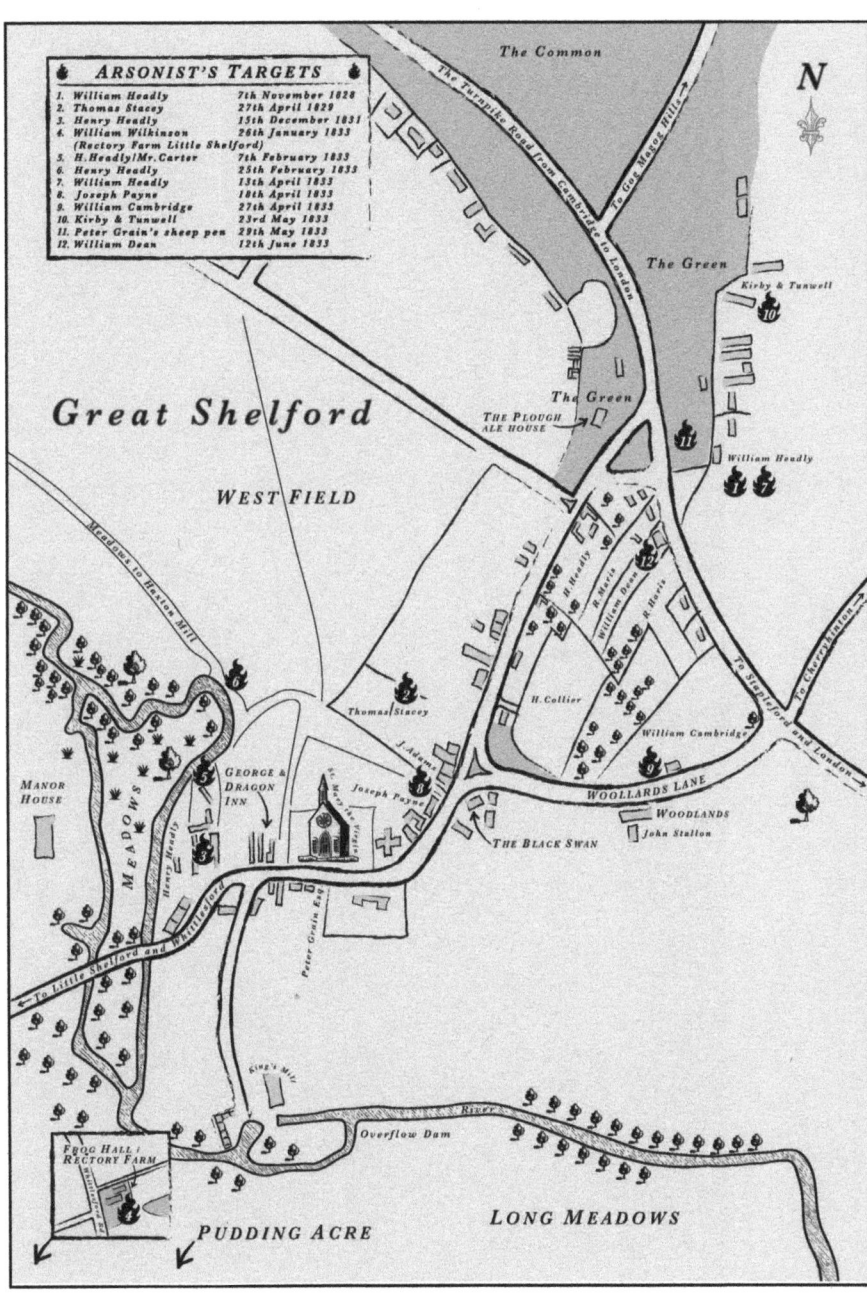

BOOK ONE

THE FIRE AT MR HEADLY'S

Chapter One

A COUPLE AND THEIR BLANKET

Red sky at night – shepherd's delight.
Red sky in the morning – farmer's barn's on fire.
Playground joke, circa 1973.

In the daytime everything that flies over Shelford is a bird or a butterfly. At night, every light in the sky is a star.

It's easy to be rosy about this. In the early nineteenth century there were no planes in the sky – just as, almost two hundred years later, the COVID-19 pandemic wiped every jet from that same, perfect blue. But some of the creatures that did fly, then as now, were not birds or butterflies but parasites. In the warmest months midges leave barely an inch of John Stallon's skin unbitten. When he rubs the bites, they run sore.

Almost as bad are damselflies and cockchafers skimming around John's head, chasing those midges for breakfast or *fourses*. And some of the 'stars' John gazes at when he and Elizabeth are alone on their evening river-walk, are dull planets. Planets only reflect light and heat. They do not generate it, like the sun, beating down on the necks of rural workers spending all their days grafting in the fields.

And sometimes the light in the sky in this part of Cambridgeshire – day or night – is fire.

★

John Stallon was born in Great Shelford – a middle-sized village about five miles from Cambridge. He was baptised at the parish church of St Mary the Virgin on December 14th, 1800. Parish records have it that John's father James Stallon was thirty-four at the time, his mother Ann (neé Fen) was the same age. This new child became the youngest of their brood; William, Ann, Jane, Henry – and John. The family were agricultural labourers, though James's brother (the original John) had found himself a trade away from the fields – as a cordwainer, or shoemaker.

Elizabeth, John's future wife, also lived her whole life in Great Shelford. In such a village, she and John must always have known each other, growing up to be workmates. And then, unexpectedly, soulmates.

Sometime in 1819 John Stallon and Elizabeth Patman are found together, laying out a blanket on Magog Down. If this is November, they might hope to see bonfires on Midsummer Common far away in Cambridge. Or if they have walked out slightly earlier, in September, it could be fireworks, at which they ooh and ahhhh – marking the end of the Fair on Stourbridge Common. Fireworks are expected – or at least hoped for – especially by young lovers, watching from a distance.

A child is conceived on one of these nights. She is baptised early the following April. The couple call their daughter Ann, for John's mother.

But wait – count back nine months. March, February, January, December…

… July. Possibly even June, a time when the city's fireworks are nowhere to be seen.

This is what I do; dream stuff up. I imagine fireworks for this couple, literal as well as metaphorical, and the literal ones immediately seem essential, meaningful.

Perhaps the child was conceived even earlier, I think. Perhaps the nine months that led to little Ann kicking and screaming her way into the world began way before June – but the couple waited a while before baptising her. Is that possible?

Possible, but unlikely. The poor in 1820, if they believe in

God at all, don't risk damning their offspring's eternal soul by allowing them to die unbaptised. There is even a special name for babies who don't survive more than a month – they are a 'Chrisom'.

A child's chances don't get much better after a month. One in three children in England at this time don't make it past five years of age.[2] Best declare your squalling infant a Christian the moment it is born – and that means baptism, asap. So, probably it really is midsummer when John and Elizabeth are spreading their blanket. That rules out fireworks completely.

It could be forks of lightening they are watching, then. The lowering thunderstorms of summer – why not? There is no blanket in a thunderstorm, just a hot press in the long grass and John's ragged coat to hold over their heads in the drenching rain.

The lightening is thrillingly out of control. It feints or strikes at trees or barns or houses dotting the countryside below the long apron-sweep of the Down. However well-framed a barn or tree, however grand the occupants of a house, lightening may strike at any time, blasting everything to flame.

It could be this that gives John the idea.

It's probable though, this particular couple are not so bold as to be out on the Down together. Hoards once gathered on the Gog-Magog hills in summer, storms permitting. They came to wrestle each other, to out-run or out-jump or out-punch each other – to out-drink each other for sure, or watch a bull being baited. These were things – whether cock-fighting or courtship – strongly disapproved of by the University Colleges. Not the running and jumping so much, but the gambling and rough crowds and loose behaviour that inevitably followed. In fact, the Gog-Magog hills are specifically mentioned when the University bans its students from such activities within a five-mile radius of the city. The Down has long had a dubious reputation.[3]

John and Elizabeth do not strike me as wild livers – the opposite; they are trying to be respectable – and their lives are a far cry from University life. He is an agricultural labourer, only nineteen. I see him as tall and wiry. She is – we know this from contemporary accounts – a very short woman, and 'twisted', a woman we would now say is 'of restricted growth', possibly disabled, though she works hard enough in the fields when there's gavelling to be done. Turn back the pages of the baptismal register – opened first at John's entry into the world – and there she is, waiting; Elizabeth Patman, daughter to John and Mary Patman, baptised in 1794. She is six years older than the quiet soul carefully courting her.

Probably, it is in a field or a barn somewhere near here – outside the village of Great Shelford but shy of the Down – that John and Elizabeth first join their imperfect bodies together. Then as now there's no particular shame in sex before marriage – the locals have a name for that, too. 'I'm not surprised those two got married, they've been bundling since last summer'.

Some of this 'bundling', from a male point of view, is about checking wares before you buy – sex, probing the guarantee of children. A poor labourer doesn't have much going for him, but a child is a mark on the world at least. 'No child, no wife' is the saying. But there's more to it for this man, perhaps.[4]

Elizabeth emerges from all that follows as a wise and stoical sort, smart – there is nothing restricted about her intelligence. But there is some uncertainty, something tentative about John. He might appreciate being with someone who is sharper, more certain than him. That said, John is outwardly steady enough. Till he is arrested, charged, tried and executed for arson he is held 'in high esteem' by the farmers in the village, his employers. The newspapers agree – he is a solid, dependable type. He just isn't much fun, probably.

From Elizabeth's point of view – leaving aside the possibility of romance, or at least a spark of anticipation – John Stallon might be her best last chance of landing a husband. Most women of Elizabeth's age – all the straight ones – were married years ago, she thinks, meaning 'straight' in the old sense, probably.

Why begrudge them romance?

Let's say tall dour John and small-but-sharp Elizabeth discover that two people, barely given a second glance by anyone else, find emotion blindsides them. A dam bursts. They are laughing as they roll apart in that barn on a field near the Down – elated! They are so pleased with themselves for having found each other (though in truth they were never far apart). I hear them giggling like idiots. And for each of them the joy is the same: a fellow human being has seen them, is drawn to them. And this 'someone' wants them in that special urgent way for which there is no substitute on God's earth – or whoever this earth currently belongs to.

Little Ann, the fruit of this odd couple's fumbling on John's ragged coat at the edge of a rutted field close by the village – is the reason that John Stallon and Elizabeth Patman marry in January 1820. They might have married anyway, since they get on so well. But sex outside marriage is one thing –a bastard (as such children are called, even in formal documents) is another. Time ticks away, Elizabeth's body sprouts new, more conventional curves, and a wedding is announced. It is consummated, as it were, on January 25 1820, and noted in the marriage register of St Mary the Virgin. By that time Elizabeth Patman – single woman of this parish – is seven months pregnant.

Sadness follows. They were right to get the baptism sorted: Ann, this treasure of theirs, is sickly from the first. Despite frantic parental prayers and so many desperate promises to each other, and despite the child desperately hanging on to life, the burial register gapes, sucking poor Ann towards it. This tiny girl slips through John and Elizabeth's fingers just seventeen months after she is born. *'From those who have little, will even that be taken away…'*

What seemed a huge boost to this odd couple's meagre prospects – delicate proof they can lead a productive life together – sinks back to the earth from whence it came.

Stlll, at least they are married now. That is some kind of advancement, some level of respectability achieved. And a shared future feels more tangible somehow, however bruised the sharers.

It is another two and a half years before a second baby is baptised; a further six years after that before a third child turns up in the baptismal register.

I wonder about that gap after the second pregnancy.

Make sure one child survives. Once that's achieved, each time the subject of 'more' arises, John fears lightening will strike a second time, punishing his levity on the Down or their lust in the field. Or perhaps he fears further bouts of childbirth will cost the tiny, twisted wife on whom he depends even more than the child she is carrying. It might cost him her life – and that has long since become unthinkable.

Poor John, to be so fearful: he needs to remind himself how tough she is.

Or are we missing something? Could it be that in the six years between their second and third child, Elizabeth suffers miscarriages? Shocks and more shocks smash away at the slow relief when that second child, John Junior, made it through his first two vulnerable years. Elizabeth may have endured more sadness than we can tell. History is full of silence where misery is concerned, especially the female kind – when it bothers to speak about women at all.

Or perhaps that's just the way it is. In an age and place before reliable birth control, babies come when babies will; this third child takes its time, that's all. Meanwhile John will accept the jokes about his name – miswritten and misspoken as John 'Stallion' his whole life. In return, he will smile that faint smile that people take for even-temperedness, or being meek, or being slow-witted – and carry on.

This third child, William – the second to survive and the last that John and Elizabeth will produce – has just reached one year of age when fires begin to flare up all around Great Shelford. John's older brother William – after whom the new child is named – gets himself killed in a pub fight, and one month later the new baby reaches the same age as poor Ann had reached when she was lost. That could be the trigger: John's steadiness – always something of a performance – is no more than the knack of not letting-on. He is winded by Bill's death – stunned by it, who wouldn't be? Burying his brother in the churchyard in December 1832, so close to the place where they let Ann's small body into the ground, is gruelling, as all burials are. Again, there is no stone for this poor family. Turves are pressed firm over the slight rise belying Bill's coffin; a bell in the church tower rings for a while, then stops ringing. Then nothing. Again. The next day, John is back-bent working the fields, battling the half-frozen, unyielding soil of Shelford.

A month later the Firestarter's 'flare-ups' flare up in earnest.

Whoever is responsible for these outrages – one barn then another, sometimes two in a day – the culprit is stealthy. Soon the rush to the engine is commonplace; the all-hands-on-deck-effort to save someone's thatch or crop from encroaching flame becomes almost normal. And John Stallon rises to the challenge. He is one of the most energetic, reliable fire-fighters in the village.

Perhaps that's why the miracle happens. The miraculous falling of suspicion on every poor man in the village, bar John himself. Some lads, deemed untrustworthy, are arrested quickly. They almost pay with their lives for no other reason than they have a loutish reputation. Others are classed as 'idiots', so they too become suspects. There is no evidence against them – how could there be? But still their grip on life is taken right to the brink before the judiciary – merciless with the guilty but hell-bent on evidence – haul these terrified souls back to safety. John Stallon sees all this and remains unsuspected. That outward steadiness comes in handy, you see.

Meanwhile, walking to the river through the fields by their cottage, or lying in their bed inside the spartan hovel they now call home, John slips his hand down and down to where Elizabeth's hand has begun to wake up her body for sex. John has discovered a new vigour in these fires; his blood is permanently up. Even Elizabeth – his small, crooked, sharp-minded and passionate soulmate, does not suspect a thing.

Or so John tells himself.

This unspoken thing between them, the curious thrill of being special – even if it's because you cause terror – settles on this couple like the downiest quilt.

Chapter Two

IN THE SWING

And the days are not full enough
And the nights are not full enough
And life slips by like a field mouse
Not shaking the grass

Ezra Pound

Shall we acknowledge the obvious? Arson is nothing new in the nineteenth century. Recently though, in the rural south, it has become the retribution of choice for numerous malcontents. Every two or three-months from 1828 to 1830, another of Cambridgeshire's barns or haulm stacks smokes, cracks and splinters into ash.

Haulm stacks – heaps of hay or pea stalks covered in thatch – are not a cash crop. This is feed to keep a farmer's livestock through the winter. Each time a stack is burned, a farmer's quest to keep his animals fed becomes that much tougher. Frustration snags the mind; anxiety smoulders. Is that steam rising from the barn's roof, backlit by the dawn or dyed blood-red at sunset? Or is it smoke? For farmers, this new, hyper-alert state-of-being is foreign, exhausting.

In 1830, rural unrest had found its sharpest focus. Workers were caught up in violent acts of sabotage as rioting swept through the villages of South-Eastern England.

Hard to believe, given the affluence of large chunks of the south today, but in comparison with the prosperous mill towns of the north of England, wages in the backward southern counties were paltry in the 1830s. Supply of labour vastly outstripped the farmers' need – especially with farm mechanisation clanking into fact. The ability of agricultural workers to find work was dwindling and with it, the workers' economic muscle. Faced with the wasting muscles of their malnourished children, some labourers determined to flex what 'muscle' they had left. They refused to work. The farmers must raise their wages. Instead of 6 shillings a week, give us eight, or eight plus beer for a family man. Farmers even now took advantage of their workers, using the mob's pressure to improve their own position. They attempted to pass on these irresistible wage demands, calling for a reduction in the tithe payments that farmers must make to the church – 10 shillings an acre in some cases. Sometimes, where farmers *did* resist the workers' calls for more beer and better money, the labourers turned to riot. Marching on a farmer's home, they demanded food and drink and threatened violence, or left notes hammered to a door. 'Pay up, or be sorry' – in the name of 'Captain Swing'.

In a few brief months, dozens of barns in the south of England were torched, and threshing machines smashed. The last were especially hated, reducing the need for hired help; another means by which farmers enriched themselves, another way (so it seemed to the labourers) to reduce once-proud workers to poverty.

The answer to the scourge of Captain Swing – so the landowners determined – was to investigate and arrest, with the emphasis on arrest; mobilise the magistrates, round up the culprits, hang the ringleaders, transport their lieutenants. Across England, 1,976 prisoners were tried; 252 were sentenced to death. Most had their sentences commuted, but nineteen men were hanged; 644 people received prison sentences, 505 people were transported, mostly to Australia. The brutality of the crackdown was deliberate and unrelenting. [5]

In the county of Cambridgeshire, its former MP Phillip Yorke, now the third Earl of Hardwicke, played a key role in this suppression. Once a liberally-minded Whig – allegedly – Hardwicke pursued a two-fold strategy. The labourers' complaints had some merit – only a fool would deny the declining condition of the hired worker. It couldn't all be down to mushrooming Beer Houses. The farmers – the Earl knew a few less-than-noble specimens – must bear some responsibility. Hardwicke launched a '*Particular enquiry into the actual state and condition of the Poor in every Parish in the county*' to be carried out by twenty named magistrates, several of them clergymen. Meanwhile the Earl – himself a significant landowner in the county – simultaneously moved to suppress what he called 'the systematic plan of the incendiaries'. With his encouragement the county's magistrates – the same magistrates who made up his inquiry team – pledged to use 'the utmost force to suppress outrage and protect property'. [6]

When the city of Cambridge caught a whiff of mobs rising in nearby villages the same month – including workers from Shelfords Great and Little – the magistrates were understandably nervous. It was said the labourers planned to march on Cambridge itself, repeating their demand for higher wages. Eight hundred 'special constables' were immediately sworn in to defend the city, while undergraduates from the university volunteered to assist by forming a troop of 'mounted yeomanry'. Beyond that, two troops of the 7th Dragoons stood by in Ipswich. [7]

In the event, the labourers turned back. Perhaps they too had heard rumours – or perhaps proof of their unequal fight was already internalised. Earlier that year, in the spring of 1830 at the city gaol at Cambridge Castle, three incendiaries – William Turner, William Reader and David Howard – had been hanged by Mr Orridge, the Prison Governor and Mr Calcraft the county executioner, at the instruction of a judge – for setting fire to farmers' barns. These outrages had taken place in the Cambridgeshire villages of Linton and Badlingham, just a few miles in each case from Cambridge, and no further distance from the Shelfords. The Judge had been unremitting when sentencing the guilty men;

You cannot expect mercy this side of the grave – you must not expect it; the gates of mercy are forever closed. [8]

And so it proved. As the *Morning Advertiser* on Weds April 7th 1830 noted of the hangings:

For the last ten years this crime has been of continual occurrence in the county, and no clue has ever been gained of the perpetrators... so that this terrible example was more than called for to warn the undiscovered miscreants of the doom awarded by the offended laws of their country.

As a strategy, it worked. Just as it had worked in 1816, and again in 1822 – the previous occasions when large-scale rioting broke out in these desperate, divided, rural parts, and power felt the urge to assert itself.

Dissatisfaction though, defies penalties. What remains in the fields and lanes of Cambridgeshire and other rural counties in the East and South of England in 1831 are watchful eyes; those alert for fires, and those looking for the opportunity to light them. When that chance is glimpsed, bingo. The blow – or the match – is struck. Sporadic fires, smashed machinery, hobbled beasts, savaged orchards – these continue as signs that hangings, transportation and hard labour may deter open riots but they do nothing to quell a labourer's sense of grievance – or the determination, somehow, to strike back.

By December 1831 Great Shelford has already experienced two such flare-ups of its own. The very first was a barn belonging to William Headly, a farmer in the village. That was as far back as the 7th of November, 1828, and the damage ran to several hundred pounds. Six months later, at the end of April 1829, a barn and haulm stack belonging to Thomas Stacey, farmer and churchwarden of St Mary the Virgin, was likewise attacked. 'And now again', the vicar Henry Finch almost certainly mutters, as smoke drifts across his churchyard. For this time, the fire starter – or starters – are even more daring.

At first light, on December 15 1831, unseen forces strike not a single, isolated barn or stack – some cowshed in a field, far from any cottage – but the farmyard at the heart of Rectory Farm, itself in the heart of Great Shelford, next door but one to the church. The firestarter is brazen – or is there a gang of them? Are they emboldened by previous triumphs, daring themselves into ever-greater risk? Or could it be a diversion? The ultimate design could be robbery for all the locals know. Some even whisper (war with France being not long over) – it could be a prelude to invasion.

Whatever the locals think (and whatever the Firestarter's intention), fire has its own ideas. Licking across the straw-strewn yard, flames consume several of Rectory Farm's well-maintained outbuildings. The victim this time – the second occasion his family's property has been targeted in the past three years – is a man named Henry Headly – a man of substance in Great Shelford, and brother to William Headly. It was William who suffered the first fire two years previously. Coincidentally, Henry Headly is John Stallon's Master – John's most regular provider of employment – though John also works for William Headly, on occasion…

Luckily for Henry Headly, the alarm is sounded by his workers, gathering at first light to receive instruction for the day. The creaking village engine is rushed from its harbour in the church, but such is the ferocity of the blaze the fire can soon be seen for miles. Insurance company tenders from Cambridge surge toward the flame. Luckily – again – the farm is close to the river; villagers line up to pass buckets of water to feed the engines and douse the heat. The fire, fierce as it is, never reaches the big house – Henry Headly's home – or, for that matter, Reverend Finch's church. But the damage is impressive.

A few hours later, flames muted to smoking whisps, Henry Headly surveys the charcoaled ghost of his cowshed. His mind will not stop reeling – or is it calculating? Soon, he will guide an insurance agent carefully around the outline of his cowshed and point out his equally ruined dairy – and shake on a settlement of £3000. [9]

Today, that would be getting on for a quarter of a million pounds.

Given this phenomenal sum, news of the fire spreads even further than its glow. People as far away as London swivel nervously in polished office chairs. We've been here before, they mutter and of course, they are thinking of Captain Swing.

For Henry Headly, in December 1831, pity for his brother's bad luck two years back has given way to something else; his smouldering farmyard confirms it. The county is again seething with malcontents, or worse.

'I'm sorry for your trouble Mr Headly'.

What's that?

'It's a mercy that no one was killed. Sir.'

The man who has dragged Henry Headly from his darkest thoughts is one of his regular, most reliable workers. Tall, gaunt, serious; not the quickest mind, but dependable, and one of the first that morning to spot the danger, raise the alarm and fetch the engine.

'Thank you John', says Headly. 'And thank you for your efforts. Here, take your money – you've got mouths to feed. There'll be no work today. Start in tomorrow'.

John Stallon nods and sets off to walk the quarter-mile to his home, exhausted and coughing. His arms and shoulders sting with the swing of many buckets, and the endless pumping of the engine has rendered his back aching and strained. His lungs, he can feel, are choked with thick smoke. But John is not downcast. Some other, more secret part of John Stallon is on fire.

Chapter Three

THE SCIENCE OF FIRE.

Spark n. a fiery particle thrown off from a fire, or alight in ashes, or produced by a flint, match etc.
Spark n. a lively young fellow.
The Concise Oxford Dictionary: the new Edition for the 1990s.

In 1831 every farmer or farm labourer knows that straw becomes more combustible when it is damp. It is, as they say, one of life's mysteries. Later, people will also know the cause of the paradox. A moisture content of 20%+ in straw produces mesolithic bacteria, a process that raises the temperature of a stack or bale to between 130°F and 140°F. The increased heat will eventually kill the mesophilic bacteria, and the straw cools. But if thermophilic bacteria take over, a rick can reach temperatures of 175°F plus.[10]

What John does understand – what he has learned recently – is that to set a barn or rick alight needs surprisingly little intervention from humanity. The spark from a flint, a bit of rag to nurse a flame, barely the breath of a child. Raising a fire is such a gentle process, but there the gentleness ends. At first the flame is puttering; before long, it's a roar. Life becomes hotter, faster – events are no longer predictable. Fire does its own thing – loosed, and lethal.

It will always be like this, John thinks, this new power of mine. Like having a firework in your head.

Chapter Four

COTTAGE COMFORTS.

A hardworking man wants at least two pints of beer a day – and his wife, especially when she suckles, ought to have one.

Esther Hewlett, *Cottage Comforts*, 1826.

The cycle ride from my home to the centre of Great Shelford takes all of five minutes – or ten, if the barrier at the railway crossing is down.

This is the first field trip I've conducted on the trail of John Stallon – the first that does not involve straining my eyes in an archive or wondering what goes on in a Firestarter's head. I have come into the village to see if I can find some trace of the cottage where John and Elizabeth Stallon lived for several years – the quiet years, before Stallon's career as arsonist ignited.

I've lived on the outskirts of the village for more than twenty-five years, so I've walked, cycled or driven past this particular house in Woollards Lane, thousands of times. All the same, it has taken many hours of poring over old maps and registers to realise this may be the place I'm looking for. Now I think I may finally have found the site of the humble worker's cottage where sometime in the 1820s, John and Elizabeth Stallon set up home.

This is what I know for sure. In 1827 a pair of tenements were put up for auction. They were owned by a farmer and carpenter called William Cambridge who lived in Woollards Lane, Great Shelford. Old Man Cambridge may even have built these tenements himself, but by 1827 he had turned seventy years old, and was not in the best of health. Looking to liquidate some of his assets and set his affairs in order, he put the small house up for sale via an advertisement in the *Cambridge Chronicle:*

To be sold by Auction by Elliot Smith.
At the Carpenter's Arms on Tuesday next, the 24th of April, 1827, at seven o'clock in the evening:
TWO COPYHOLD TENEMENTS occupied by James Wright and John Stallion; with a COMMON RIGHT over the valuable Common of Great Shelford.
Also ONE ACRE (more or less) of SWARD or ORCHARD, well planted with Apple, Pear, and Walnut Trees; and FIFTY small ASH, ELM, POPLAR, & WILLOW TREES, and 100 SPIRES; now growing on the premises.
Land-Tax 3s; Quit-Rent 1s 6d.
For Particulars enquire of WILLIAM CAMBRIDGE.[11]

To discover the house you are renting is being sold by the landlord is tough, even if, as Old Cambridge ensured in his advertisement, the sitting tenants are named. Labourers like James Wright and John Stallon had little in the way of security either of income or employment, and now their homes were being sold over their heads.

Unfortunately, there are two vital bits of information missing from the advert which make it difficult to get any accurate sense of the impact this change had on John and Elizabeth – or even work out exactly where the houses stood.

First – obviously – it does not tell us who bought the house; could the incoming landlord be counted on to be more or less sympathetic to his tenants? For quite a few weeks I try to track records of the sale via papers that might have been left by the auctioneer, Elliot Smith, or by William Cambridge himself. A bill of sale? Or deeds to the property? I can find nothing.

Secondly, and perhaps more surprising, the advertisement makes no mention of the location of the cottage; except that it is in Great Shelford, I have no idea of the address.

The house's whereabouts would have remained a mystery, were it not for the detective work of a young woman called Fanny Lucretia Wale, from the neighbouring village of Little Shelford. She, I discover, was on the trail of John and Elizabeth Stallon almost exactly one hundred years before me – and only ninety years after the events we are interested in.

In the early years of the twentieth century Fanny Wale – daughter of a wealthy local family – became Shelford's very own 'Edwardian Lady'. Unlike Edith Holden's famous 'Diary…', Fanny's illustrated book – *A Record of Shelford Parva* – is part nature diary, part social history. It was compiled from evidence gathered on Fanny's frequent walks around the neighbourhood, and from her house-to-house enquiries. It's hard not to smile at the thought of the locals responding to this gentlewoman's naively intrusive questions; how many live in your cottage?! What rent do you pay? And do you have other children? Questions about whose relative is related to whom, and how they came to live in the village in the first place. All this Fanny dutifully notes in her diary. The book was published locally in 2012, complete with Fanny's beautiful drawings. [12]

Though setting out to compose a history of her own village, Fanny clearly develops a fascination for one particular bit of gossip that comes her way on these home visits – an obsession just as gripping as my own. The detailed sketch map of the two villages included in her book is complete with annotations cataloguing the targets of 'John Stallion, the Shelford Arsonist'.

Fanny's grip on the facts is not always secure: to begin with, she dates the fires to 1841, rather than a decade earlier. In this I suspect she may have been misled by elderly villagers anxious to present themselves as eyewitnesses. A ninety-year old in 1920 could credibly report events in the 1840s in dramatic, personally-recalled detail. If those events occurred ten years earlier, less so. Fanny also refers to John as a nightwatchman. Nonetheless, she marks the house of 'John Stallion' on her map, and reports that the cottages were shielded from view by another, larger house – clearly still in existence at the time she was writing. This house, she says, was called *Woodlands*. A book in the village library reveals that *Woodlands*-as-was still stands almost exactly opposite the library – right there, on Woollards lane.

I already know that Great Shelford's land was finally Enclosed in 1835 (a massive upheaval in the local community, as we'll learn). At that time, a map was drawn detailing the confirmed ownership of all the land in the village. Looking up that map in the Cambridgeshire Archive in Ely I had seen that the patch of land corresponding to the place where *Woodlands* stands was owned by someone whose name is split inconveniently across a crease in the map, and so remains completely illegible. After consulting with staff at the Archive and spending some time passing a magnifying glass between us, we finally agreed the name comprises an initial – T. followed by a surname beginning with W. This last name ended with an 's', while the penultimate letter seemed to be an 'r'.

Next, we pulled out the Enclosure register. This enormous ledger carries an entry for this same patch of land 'with houses and gardens', the copyhold of which is attributed to a Thomas Willers.

We now had the buyer of the property and thus, John and Elizabeth's new landlord – assuming, as seems likely, Willers bought the place at the auction organised by Elliot Smith on behalf of William Cambridge in 1827, rather than from an intermediary owner.

There is no surviving record of Great Shelford's 1831 census, but later I will drag out further details about Willers from the surveys of 1841 and 1851 – and this provides some fascinating information, for Willers is no ordinary character.

Meanwhile, I lock up my pushbike outside the library and cross the road to knock on the door of a house now badged as 3A Woollards Lane. I am ready to take the next step in my pursuit of John and Elizabeth Stallon.

★

Warned of my visit by email, Stephen West opens his front
door and invites me inside. Stephen has the air of a man on
a mission. Number 3A as it happens, is exactly that.

Stephen immediately confirms that in times gone by
this house and its semi-detached neighbour were one large
house called 'Woodlands'. The half that comprises Stephen's
home was then part house, part outbuildings. In fact,
Stephen is the new owner: he has not even moved in yet.
The reason quickly becomes apparent. What is essentially
a Georgian house with a barn attached is currently half-
building site, half-book repository – stacked to the rafters
with old furniture, dusty bags of plaster, and dustier reading
matter.

Until he passed away eighteen months before, Stephen's
father Richard lived here. Richard was a notable geologist
studying his subject to the last, but in the cold, uninsulated
house, he gradually withdrew to a single room warmed by
a single gas fire. All around, his elegant furniture and the
five grandfather clocks he'd collected over years must have
shivered in sympathy.

Now that the house is his responsibility, Stephen has set
about renovating the place with a vengeance. The challenge
he tells me, is achieving a decent level of environmental
efficiency while doing his best to conserve the original
features of the house.

As I follow Stephen from room to room, I wonder how
much he knows about the role this house – or the land it
stands on – played in the spate of arson attacks that terrorised
our village almost two hundred years ago. Great Shelford
likes to keep its secrets veiled.

At the time of my visit, 3A has several distinct parts.
The largest component, butting up against No 3 is clearly
part of the original *Woodlands* – a long, narrow, two storey

house facing the lane and now subdivided. On the right-hand end of the house as we face it is a one-story section, providing a front door through which I have just entered. This construction forms a passage between the oldest part of the house and a much newer one-storey section which stands end-on to the road, and runs south to north – that is, perpendicular to the old part of the house, to the passageway, and to the lane outside. This in turn links to a very interesting-looking two-to-three storey building tucked in behind. I have stared at the roof of this part of Stephen's new home several times, both from the road and from a nearby carpark. It has what I have thought of till now as Dutch eves, but according to Stephen is referred to by builders as a Mansard roof. Before today, I've not been able to see enough of this part of the house to really work out how old it is.

Stephen very kindly makes us both a mug of tea and we complete the guided tour of the ground floor, with my host pointing out sections that his father built in the 1950s, cleverly tying together all the disparate parts of the property. The part I'm really interested in though, is that rear section – the part that is perpendicular to the main house, with a roof that looks like it might just be the work of a farmer/carpenter at the turn of the nineteenth century.

That may well be so. We tip into the garden, and it's obvious that this section must at one time have been a barn – there is a hayloft, and a loading bay on the first floor. My theory that William Cambridge may have been the builder is looking good. Yet oddly, there are two front doors providing entrance from the garden side of the building. Does this suggest it was once comprised two cottages? In terms of age, we seem on fairly safe ground: Stephen tells me that a tiler who worked on the roof identified the single-peg tiles he was replacing as among the first in the UK to be machine-produced – dating the building to around the 1870s.[13] If the tiles were added to an existing roof, the building could be much older.

Things get less positive as we continue the tour inside. The building has undoubtedly done time as a stable-cum-carriage house. We pass a saddle rest by one of the front doors and enter a tack room inside. There are numerous other indications that this was once used as a house for horses, rather than people. Fanny Wale tells us that in the early twentieth century, *Woodlands* was owned by a Dr Magoris – a prosperous man. The 1911 census shows that the good doctor had two servants living in the house, as well as his wife and two daughters. Probably, he kept a carriage and horses. Only since the 1950s Stephen tells me, has the Magoris horse-haven been converted into a more suitable space for humans.

Two sequences of development seem possible. Workers' cottages were usually much more basic in construction than this, almost certainly single story. Perhaps the barn-then-stable was built when those simple cottages were cleared away, or perhaps Dr Magoris made his coach house by extending the tenement walls upwards.

More likely, the tenements were further distant from the *Woodlands*, tucked away deeper into the orchard mentioned in the sales ad. If so, they are lost to us, lying beneath a street called Spinney Drive that now curls its way behind Woollards Lane, cutting off William Cambridge's 'sward' at the knees.

And yet, back in the garden, the two entrances stare back at me. There is a large fireplace in the end wall of the 'barn' which looks original, rather than being a later addition; it seems an odd thing to have in a coachhouse and certainly a barn. Could William Cambridge have set out to build a barn, then decided accommodation for workers was a more pressing need? The word 'tenement' used in the original advertisement usually implies multiple occupation of a single building…

I look back into the barn/house from the outside, leaning forward, squinting into what might, just might have been Elizabeth's only downstairs room – long before Dr Magoris decided it was better fit for horses. Almost two centuries and a good deal of lost history fog the space between us. The only thing I have by way of a torch, is imagination.

*

Elizabeth Stallon (neé Patman) has poured herself a cup of beer, even though it is only morning. The sound of the alarum rings in her ears, while clouds of dense smoke thicken the sky above the cottage. Elizabeth, heavy-bellied, tries hard to catch her breath, as if she herself had been working in the fields and then run, lungs bursting, to pass buckets of river water fast and faster to quench the fire feeding on Rectory Farm.

In fact, Elizabeth has not worked in the fields for some time. The birth of her second child, a full seven years ago – taught her that strapping an infant to her back and trying to walk to the fields, let alone work in them is – for her already disadvantaged body – impossible. Once that child, John Jr was old enough to be left with a neighbour, she was free again. She went harvesting for the next five summers. But not this year. John has insisted; for both their sakes – this time the baby must stick. The arduous plod behind her husband, gathering the bundles he cut with his sickle, is passed, in the harvest of 1831, to John Jnr. The boy – JJ, he would doubtless be called today – was seven years of age by this time. Young, but labourers' children in Shelford learn quickly if they wanted to eat. John Junior, skinny as a rake and as serious minded as his father (if that were possible), could eat for England.

Seeing the boy return with John at the end of his day of 'gavelling', fingers torn, so tired and pleased with himself, would make any mother proud. Elizabeth also felt irked.

Loathe as she is to admit it, Elizabeth has missed the open air and high spirits of harvest. She almost misses the constant jibes about her size, though being so much closer to the ground never in fact makes the work any easier. Since realising she is pregnant again, and John being so determined, she has been a prisoner in the house. Lately, looking around, bored of the cottage walls, she's had space to imagine a different, more outdoorsy future. The cottage is rented and comes with a Right of Commons – that is, the right to use the village common lands for grazing (among other things like collecting wood or digging gravel). Not that John and Elizabeth have much to graze. The only livestock they have amassed in ten years of hard work and marriage are two ducks that peck around in the scrappy orchard attached to the cottage. Recently though, John's thinking has been more expansive. They have talked about getting a sheep or even – John's dream – a pig. According to *The Labourer's Friend* – a magazine many farmers read, along with a few gifted workers like John – a pig costs almost nothing to keep. Once purchased, it feeds on scraps and is thus the best choice for the working man. Meanwhile, in between looking for the ducks and spotting their blue-green eggs in the grass, Elizabeth has taken in washing.

Even here, pregnancy – and as always, her lack of height – are issues to overcome.

The average washing line won't work for Elizabeth. To sling the line low so she can reach it – without wobbling her way skywards on a set of steps – means clothes pegged to the line muddy themselves long before a prop can be jerked into place. The answer, when she discovers it, is simple.

William Cambridge – the Stallons' landlord till a few years ago – was once a carpenter as well as a farmer. Old Cambridge shows John how to employ a pulley, of the kind Cambridge himself once used to use to raise the massive joists of a barn or house – perhaps even, the joists of this house. Now the line stretches from the upstairs window of the cottage, across the yard, to an answering block fastened high in the elm tree. The sheets on the line, Old Cambridge proclaims, now hang high and handsome. All Elizabeth has to do, is drag her basket of washing – carefully, a little at a time – up to the first floor of the cottage.

These days, Elizabeth does not even attempt it herself. Instead, she calls out to her neighbour, Sarah Walker, for help. The Sarah of old would easily have been bribed with the hold of a baby. Now, with John Jr so far grown, and the impending baby so far along, Sarah will forego the bribe. Elizabeth waits while Sarah obligingly carries the basket up the stairs to what was once a hayloft. Then the two women gossip while Elizabeth leans carefully from the window and pegs the washing onto the 'filling line'. She then pulls on the other, 'returning line', and the wet clothes and sheets feed haltingly across the yard, to flap energetically in the breeze.

For a while this new line is a godsend. Then one day Sarah, a small shrewish woman not much taller than Elizabeth – though better proportioned and poker-backed – hints this neighbourly co-operation will soon end. Sarah and James have a 'surprise' of their own coming, and Sarah doubts the stairs will be so easy for her then.

Elizabeth stares at her neighbour; she doesn't want to upset the older woman – especially now the new system is in play. But Sarah giving birth? She is at least forty-five by Elizabeth's reckoning. Nor will John be impressed with news that Elizabeth wants to drag washing up the stairs again. Bad enough his wife has to bend over to scrub and rinse the clothes, though the pennies she earns are useful enough.

Elizabeth smiles as kindly – and as conclusively – as she can. 'That's good news for you, Sarah', she says.

Elizabeth does not mention this conversation to John. Nor does she comment a few weeks later, when Sarah sets off in her best clothes to visit a relative in Royston and returns the following day with a baby son.

Now, when Elizabeth sits to catch her breath at the top of the stairs and frets at the stirring of the baby inside, Sarah has her own baby gurgling in her arms. The new mother is ready to inform Elizabeth yet again that this child is so bonny compared with poor, spindly John Junior. But then, there's not an inch of fat on Elizabeth.

No wonder she finds it difficult to carry a child the full distance.

Chapter Five

A CHANGE OF HANDS

Folks in Shelford and those parts –
Have twisted lips and twisted hearts.

Rupert Brooke

James Wright somehow gets himself over to the *Carpenter's Arms* on the evening of the 24 April, 1827, even though the pub is far away, in Cambridge. James wants to witness his fate, even though he has no control over it, for today is the day when the cottages are to be auctioned. John Stallon, his neighbour, has no such desire to know the future. John stays home, steadily scraping the mud off his boots with his vicious-looking reaping hook. But when James returns, late at night and several pints of ale to the good, John cannot help himself. He slips out to meet his neighbour in the yard.

'Some sheep farmer', James says, in answer to John's question. 'Claiming kin with them trees'.

John waits impatiently, while the older man weeps with laughter, enjoying his joke. Finally, James is able to speak.

'It's him bought it; that's yer landlord. Him out front. The shepherd, Willows'.

John Stallon is not the only man in the village whose name is always misspelt, or misspoken. Thomas Willers – or Willows – is the shepherd in question. Around this time – as we know from the census – he bought the *Woodlands*, the long skinny house at the front of the plot. Its front door opens almost directly on to the Lane, and it hides the workers' cottages from passers-by. Willers bought the big house and moved in with his growing family. And now he has captured the copyhold of the tenements in which the Wrights and the

Stallons live, and captured the orchard that goes with them, too. He has a whole little estate to command.

If he really is a shepherd, Thomas Willers is an unusual one, though he registers himself as such in the Juror Book for Great Shelford in 1830. Later still, as the 'sward or orchard' begins to fill with assorted piles of ironmongery and horse-harnesses, with old doors and boots and meat-hooks and panes of precious glass, Willers lists himself more accurately in the census as a 'Dealer' (1841), or 'Jobber' (1851). There is clearly money to be made in buying and selling – so much so, that from the start Willers can afford to neglect the orchard. He doesn't even object to Elizabeth's ducks scratching around in the yard. No surprise there, since he lets his own raucous children bounce on the limbs of apple trees till the branches snap – much to John's quiet fury. Still, it does at least turn out that Willers is content to let his inherited tenants stay put. All he cares, is that the rent on the cottages is paid; for him, it's a steady little income stream, requiring minimal effort.

Shoot forward, and the 1861 census reveals that Willers has changed trades again, and is now running *Woodlands* as a pub. The man though, remains the same. A news item in the Cambridge Independent Press dated April 29, 1865, reports that Thomas Willows, beerhouse keeper, has been fined by the magistrate for serving drinks on a Sunday – outside the permitted hours. He calls his pub, rather knowingly, *The Ancient Shepherd*.

After the cottages change hands in 1827, it seems John Stallon blames not Willers, a man from outside the village, for the ruin of the fruit trees and the hobbling of the orchard, or for the neglect of the 'estate'. Instead, pulleys or no, John holds Old Man Cambridge responsible for his declining lot. The selling of the tenements feels to John like a betrayal, and this will eventually incur his revenge – of a particularly fiery kind.

Chapter Six

OTHER JOHNS WHO CAN READ.

....who would hinder a poor Man from keeping an Ewe and Lamb, or if he can compass one, a little Heifer? For these can run upon a Green, or among the Lanes and Highways, till the Crop be ended; and then away with them into the common Fields...and by this Advantage in some Places divers poor Families are in good Part sustained.

Letter from 'Apuleius' to *Northampton Mercury*,
17 October, 1726.

John could have taken his wheezing lungs home from Mr Headly's farm on the day of the fire in December 1831. To do that, he would turn right just beyond the church, walk along Woollards Lane for three hundred yards, then duck behind the house called Woodlands. That would fetch him up at the cottage he shares with his wife Elizabeth and their son John Jr, next door to James and Sarah Walker, and their own 'miraculous' young son. Today instead he spurns the opportunity to turn right and keeps walking along the High Street. John is enjoying the freedom of a few hours release from work – and the exhilaration of a third fire set without detection. The rewards for his efforts in yet again dousing a fire he himself caused, jangle in his pocket.

Walking in this direction, towards the village of Trumpington in the north, he will pass the *Black Swan Inn* (known by locals as the 'Dirty Duck'). He will pass too the thatched pub called *The Square and Compasses*, and beyond that, a new beer house called *The Plough*. Maybe later. For now, John walks to one of his favourite places – a once-stout gate beyond which the meadows of the village Commons stretch from the edge of Great Shelford all the way to Trumpington. He likes to watch the animals, mooching about in the grass and occasionally looking up, noticing him. He dreams that he might own some livestock one day – more than a couple of ducks, anyway.

In John's pocket is a scrap of paper, covered in words.

The chief evidence that John Stallon can read is – you might think ironically – drawn from the sermon given at his funeral. John lies dead in his box at the front of the church. What the Rev Edward Baines, Fellow of Christ's College, delivers to the congregation of St. Mary the Virgin on a bleak Sunday morning in December 1833 – cannot be called a eulogy. Instead, Baines unleashes upon the battered hearts of the family, neighbours and shame-faced friends of 'John Stallion' an unrelenting diatribe on the justice of John's execution, and the non-existent hope of mercy for those who die impenitent. Whether the notes introducing the published version of the sermon are also the work of this 'good reverend' we can't be sure. The copy I track down in the Cambridgeshire Collection – the archive housed at the Central Library in Cambridge – doesn't definitively say. The author does though make it very clear that John Stallon's literacy must not be regarded as a redeeming achievement. Far from it. Rather, it is proof of his wickedness. Society has been good to Stallon; even he, an unskilled labourer, has been able to unlock the mystery of words. It can only be John's personal wickedness that leads him to repay his society with the barbarous destruction of property. It does not occur to the Reverend (or his editor) that a grasp of words – this potential access to new ideas from outside the village – might cause a person to question the existing order of things, or to yearn for something better than grinding poverty. The author or authors of this funeral pamphlet are so rammed full of holy indignation, it stifles all their Christian empathy.

How Stallon managed to snag the opportunity to educate himself is admittedly mysterious. There would be no National School in Great Shelford until 1843, and the British School – catering for non-conformists – would not follow till twenty-seven years after that. There were schools for both boys and girls before then – so called Dame schools – but the education these offered was meagre and Dame schools were fee-paying. Those labourers' children that did enrol would frequently be absent, especially during harvest. By their early teens, most children were entirely swallowed up by the adult world of work.

So how on earth did John Stallon become literate? One possibility is that the parish church of St Mary the Virgin, marker of all the stages of Stallon's life – baptism, marriage, bereavements and his own pitiful funeral – also played a hand in his education. There is plenty of precedent for this. Sunday schools taught children like John to read so they could follow the prayer book or sing in the choir. Less formally, a minister, spotting a child with ability, might take it upon himself to teach the child its letters.

This is what may have happened to another John – John Denson, a self-styled 'peasant-farmer' living in Waterbeach, a village exactly as far to the north of Cambridge as Great Shelford is to the south. Denson was already a man of thirty-one when Stallon was born, but like our John, John Denson was born into the class of agricultural labourers and was unusual among them in developing the ability to read and write.

Like Stallon, Denson also worked in the fields during the era of Enclosure. In this radical shakeup of land distribution, the chief landowners of a village agreed to swap scattered parcels of land for a more focussed holding near their homestead. Hedgerows formerly required to divide the small strips of earth by which parity was maintained in the old system, were ripped out, and new hedges – the fastest growing being hawthorn or 'quicks' – were planted to create the borders of much larger fields. This was no small project; in the peak enclosure years in England – 1750-1850 – more miles of hedge were planted (about 200,000 miles, in fact) than in the previous half-millenium.[14]

The alleged aim of these larger fields was to make farming more efficient. In the process, and to make this new allocation of land palatable to all the farmers, the total cake of land was increased by the absorption of the Commons and the 'waste' land that typically surrounded every village. True, Great Shelford itself was not enclosed until 1835 – two years after Stallon's death – but Enclosure was certainly in the Shelford air in 1831. The parish was in fact lagging far behind Denson's Waterbeach, which had enclosed all its lands by 1809. Great Shelford was even an island in the Thriplow Hundred: the adjoining parishes of Stapleford (1814) Whittlesford (1809) Trumpington (1801-9) and Little Shelford (1814) had all seen their Commons soaked up years before and redistributed with the consequent loss of Right of Commons formerly enjoyed by the poor. Only Thriplow itself (1840) held out longer than Great Shelford.

Labourers in enclosed parishes no longer had the right to graze sheep or cows on the village green while the Commons, whose grazing meadows were formerly shared by rich and poor, had vanished. Stallon would have been keenly aware of the impact this was having on neighbouring villages – and villagers – and aware too that the idea of enclosing Shelford's Commons – over which he now stared, enjoying his leisure and dreaming of sheep (or maybe a pig) – was being hotly discussed and plotted by the village farmers – the Masters who paid John's diminishing wages.

Intrinsically linked with the push for Enclosure was reform of the Poor Law. The New Poor Law Act came into force in 1834. Prior to this time, labourers who fell on hard times could in theory boost their family's diet with milk from beasts fed on the Commons. They were entitled to fuel their fires with wood gathered from the Commons. They could also apply to the parish for relief funds. These were drawn from tithes paid by farmers and were distributed in exchange for menial labour. After Enclosure, these tithes were much reduced, and with the advent of the New Poor Law 'paupers' must seek either indoor or outdoor relief – both of which exacted hours and days of punitive labour in exchange. This was no accident, for the principle of 'less eligibility' was now in force; life for those inside the workhouse *must* be harder than the life of ordinary workers outside, in order to ward off their moral decline.

For John Denson, witness to the Enclosure of Waterbeach, the impact was devastating. He was forced on more than one occasion to seek relief from the parish himself, and he felt the demeaning nature of it keenly;

From going out as a jobbing gardener, and from the profits arising from my small garden, I continued, though with difficulty, to support myself and family; except on one or two occasions, when, for a few days, I had to work at the gravel pits; and I can assure my readers that, setting aside the degrading necessity of it, it is not very pleasant work at them, in cold weather, with a hungry belly, and a growling overseer to visit you. [15]

The Waterbeach Denson remembers before Enclosure seems almost like Eden in comparison; the annexing of the Commons by private landowners was as good as theft.

Denson's reaction – using the powers his literacy gave him, the experience he'd gained from his work as a gardener, and the energy of his Methodist faith – was to consider how the rural economy could be reorganised in a more equitable way. Currently, every destitute labourer was eligible to receive funds from the parish in return for menial work such as breaking rocks in the gravel pits, or mending roads. But what if instead every parish had land set aside for the relief of the poor? Every worker in distress could be allotted, for a small annual rent, an acre of land or – if that was too much to ask – half an acre. On this land the worker and his family could grow potatoes or corn as Denson himself had learned to do. No expensive machinery was required; the soil could be tilled with a spade rather than a plough. This ensured the cultivation was sympathetic to the land and that crops grown were for subsistence of the pauper's family; this was not intended to be a commercial venture. By these means men and women could become genuine peasants – a term Denson approved of. It implied that a good part of a person's livelihood was gained by working their own modest piece of land. Wouldn't this save villagers from the demeaning life of the labourer, forever dependent on landowning Masters for work, or on the 'charity' of the parish when the work ran out?

Denson's writing on the subject was collected in a single volume in 1830 and published as *A Peasant's Voice to Landowners*. Its original form though, was a series of letters to the *Cambridge Chronicle* beginning in 1819, and after 1821, published in a new journal called *The Labourers' Friend and Handicrafts' Chronicle*.

I imagine these articles filtering down to John Stallon via back copies. Stallon's one-time landlord, the farmer/ carpenter William Cambridge still lived just across the road from *Woodlands* cottage. Perhaps copies of *The Labourer's Friend* were smuggled out of the old man's house by William's daughter-in-law (and Elizabeth Stallon's best friend) Sarah Cambridge. Once acquainted with Denson's ideas, John is reluctant to surrender them – so charged are they with the possibility of change. By the light of a lamp in the cottage, he carefully folds a page of the journal into a crease, and with his pocketknife sharpened to a razor's edge, separates the page. He slips it – folded once more – into the sagging pocket of his work-coat.

Or it may be that a newspaper cutting of an entirely different kind has found its way into John's pocket – a news item from *The Bury and Norwich Post*, bearing the name of another literate labourer who shares the name of John – the poet, John Clare:

A Northamptonshire peasant named J. Clare, has lately published
a volume of poems, which evince considerable talent. The Marquis of
Exeter has granted him an annuity of £15 per annum, and other
friends of rising genius have taken him by the hand, and by their
bounty rendered him comfortable for life.[16]

Anyone aware of how the life of John Clare panned out will
bridle at the phrase 'comfortable for life'. Like John Stallon
and John Denson, John Clare's life was one traumatised by
Enclosure – and complicated as much as enriched by literacy.
For John Clare, the peasant poet, this conflict ended in insanity.

Seven years John Stallon's senior, Clare grew up in the
village of Helpstone, then a part of Northamptonshire, but
today mapped firmly on the Cambridgeshire side of the
border.

Clare's father was, like the fathers of both Denson and
Stallon, an agricultural labourer – in his case a thresher. As a
young man, Clare worked in the fields, but also, until the age
of eleven or twelve, he attended a Dame school in Helpstone
for just four months in the year. From this slender opportunity
John Clare became literate, and the world of books, and
particularly poetry, sprang open to him. Very quickly, he was
writing his own verse, remarkable for its detailed depictions
of the nature he encountered in the countryside around
Helpstone. His first collection, *Poems Descriptive of Rural Life*
and Scenery, was a huge success, selling 3000 copies in its first
year. This compared very favourably with his contemporary
Keats' fortune when his first collection *Lamia,* sold just 500
copies.[17] Picked up in literary circles Clare was lauded as the
'peasant poet', and he briefly became the toast of London.

But whereas the early poems were praised for their forensic
observation of the natural world, Clare's later verse becomes
increasingly focussed on the destructive impact of changes in

the rural economy:

> Enclosure like a Buonaparte let not a thing remain
> It levelled every bush and tree and levelled every hill
> And hung the moles for traitors – though the brook is
>   running still
> It runs a naked stream cold and chill
> $\qquad\qquad\qquad\qquad$ *Rememberances*[18]

> ...birds and trees and flowers without name
> All sighed when lawless Law's enclosure came
> And dreams of plunder in such rebel schemes
> Have found too truly they were but dreams
> $\qquad\qquad\qquad\qquad$ *The Mores*[19]

Clare had written about Swordy Well – a favourite playground from his childhood – as early as 1820, 'I loved thee Swordy Well, and love thee still'. But soon his identification with this ancient stone quarry and the plants that live there is even more intense, to the extent that he assumes its voice, and feels its pain:

> I'm Swordy Well, a piece of land
> That's fell upon the town
> Who worked me till I couldn't stand
> And crush me now I'm down.
> $\qquad\qquad\qquad\qquad$ *The Lament of Swordy Well* [20]

The damage caused by Enclosure is, in Clare's eyes, similarly all-consuming. The re-directed waterways, new fences and 'keep out' signs that naturally follow the assertion that this is now private property, prevent landless peasants from wandering. A walk across fields has become trespass; literally, peasants may no longer follow the flight of their fancy. This in turn robs the poor of their communion with the plants and trees, wildlife, and the domesticated animals they formerly encountered there. Second, the intensive cultivation that Enclosure permits robs former Common land like Swordy Well of its role as safe harbour for fauna and flora – and people:

I've scarce a nook to call my own
For things that creep or flye
The beetle hiding 'neath a stone
Does well to hurry by
[…]
There was a time my bit of ground
Made freemen of the slave
The ass no pindard dare to pound
When I his supper gave

The gipseys camp was not affraid
I made his dwelling free
Till vile enclosure came and made
A parish slave of me

The Lament of Swordy Well

Finally, and less obvious to a modern atomised sensibility, the loss of commons deprives the village of the communal activities, games, and even work that once played a vital part in enriching the social lives of its inhabitants. These things Clare feels keenly as the loss of his childhood and a diminution of his vital adult self; it is the loss of the country workers' entire way of life.

The physical expulsion from this rural idyll is mirrored in Clare's case by intellectual alienation from the people he grew up with. This begins with him finding his identity as a poet – setting him apart from his labouring classmates. It only grows with his new status as a poetic wonder. Both are grounded in and made possible by his ability to read and write. In 1822 he writes to his publisher:

'I live here among the ignorant like a lost man…'[21]

But Clare's sudden elevation did not last. As the market for poetry collapsed in favour of the emerging English novel, Clare found himself struggling to get published and couldn't earn enough to feed his family. The burden of this economic struggle was compounded by Clare's frustration at finding himself dismissed in London as a nine-day wonder. Whether this was a causal force, or merely coincidental, a mental depression was growing that would lead Clare to be admitted to an asylum in Essex where he would stay for four years. Both the carefree seasons of his childhood and the wonder of his public acclaim were long gone – and Clare identifies with another suffering aspect of nature:

> For summer is the season; even then the little fly
> Finds friends enow, indeed, both for leisure and for play;
> But on the winter window, it must crawl alone to die:
> Such is life and such am I, a wounded and a winter-stricken
>   fly
>
> *The Old Man's Song*[22]

After he 'escaped' from the asylum and walked home to Helpstone in a deluded state, friends and supporters of this 'winter-stricken fly' banded together to secure Clare the tenancy of a cottage with land. The plan was, that by cultivating this small piece of land – which sounds a suitably 'mindful' activity – Clare would be able to support himself while giving his mind some ease. About this change Clare is initially optimistic:

'I am going from Helpstone at Spring to a cottage at Northbro'
– where I hope that exercise will keep one in health and then I will
have a path to contentment…'[23]

And why shouldn't Clare be optimistic? This is the very

recipe John Denson and his supporters had long been prescribing for the rural poor. John Denson himself had been successfully practising what he preached for half a lifetime.

Sadly for Clare, the shift to Northborough – though only a matter of three miles from Helpstone – prised Clare from the micro-world with which he was familiar. He felt his exile from Helpstone – even a Helpstone distorted by Enclosure – as an unbreachable rift. He would spend the last twenty-three years of his life in the asylum at Northampton. His poems protesting about Enclosure, though written in the decade before John Stallon leans on his gate, will lie among Clare's papers, unpublished for more than a century.[24]

It could be news of Clare's fame or his early poems relishing nature – or John Denson's radical ideas about peasant farming that John Stallon reaches for as he stands at the gate to Great Shelford's Commons. Or it occurs to me that if there is a piece of paper in his pocket that day, it may not be reading matter at all.

Stallon's incendiarism that morning may have won him not the opportunity to read, but to write. What if the scrap in his pocket is not a printed page ripped from a journal or pamphlet, but a plain piece of rough paper scrounged from a worker at the paper mill in Sawston, three miles from Shelford? Here is a space for John Stallon to set his thoughts – stirred by his own Clare-like encounters with nature – or maybe to express his feelings about the impending Enclosure of Great Shelford, in verse or essay form. It could even be that Stallon's mind is so fired with images from the dramatic burning of the barns at Rectory Farm that he might distil them into his own, stumbling verse.

Neither John Denson, nor John Clare ever pulled off that feat – to capture the world as it looks to the incendiary. Clare does refer to the then rampant attacks of arsonists in a private letter. In 1831, just six months before John Stallon strikes at Mr Headly's farm, Clare writes to a friend that he 'never saw so terrible a threatening of rev[o]lutionary forbodings as there were maschine breaking & grain destroying mania of last winter' – the winter of Captain Swing.[25] Clare's 'forboding' is rooted in his fear of the mob, and distrust of those who manipulate it – so real to him, even while, in the very month that Stallon's flames destroy Mr Headly's haulm stack, the poet writes to his correspondent again, saying 'I am no politician but I think a reform is wanted…' But he never writes poetry directly about arson, or enters the mind of the arsonist as he does the 'mind' of the quarry at Swordy Well.

For that we have to turn to one final writer from the labouring class. Inconveniently given the title of this chapter, this is a man named James.

James Reynolds Withers was born twelve years after John Stallon, in Weston Colville, a Cambridgeshire village twelve miles from Great Shelford. His father was a cordwainer or shoemaker – just like John Stallon's uncle. James Withers' father died in poverty when Young Jim was a child. At first, ten-year-old James got work with a farmer. Then, luckily, his mother managed to get her boy apprenticed to the man who had taken over her late husband's business, such as it was. Sadly, James' mother died soon after, and the hoped-for job at the end of the apprenticeship failed to materialise. James was forced to set up on his own in the nearby village of Fordham, while wielding a reaping hook at harvest time to make ends meet. When even that failed, Withers took his young family into the workhouse in order to avoid a plunge into debt. His real luck however, was to have had a mother who taught him to read and write. Like Clare before him, Withers found he had a gift for poetry:

'…in all my occupations I found scattered some lines of poetry. In winter, if I shivered at my task, there was the beautiful hoar frost on the hedge to admire…in the busy toiling harvest there was poetry in the lines of sheaves, and even in the poppied stubble.'[26]

Again like John Clare before him, James Withers was

'discovered' as an authentic voice of the countryside – and his career as a poet took off. Predictably enough, that career followed a similar trajectory to Clare's. Withers was well-published and travelled widely in the UK, and even beyond – and was then quietly forgotten. Having a trade to fall back on, however humble, clearly helped James to weather the storms of rejection and times of little that followed. Unlike Clare, he was able to live most of his life as a free man – but like Clare, he kept writing. Wither's poem, *The Song of the Incendiary* is probably as close as it is possible to get to John Stallon's mindset that cold, overcast December morning at the end of 1831 after he had set the fire at Rectory Farm:

When the wind is loud, and the night is dark,
And the village is hush'd in the arms of sleep,
And no one near my steps to mark,
Then away from my home I slyly creep:
To the barn I glide,
On the windward side,
Where the roof slopes low with its crispy thatch:
There's no one near;
There's nought to fear,
And now for the coal or the silent match.
'Tis done, 'tis done, and the flames ascend;
Wider they spread and higher they rise:
Then stealthily home my course I bend,
While the red glow lights the surrounding skies
And I join in the throng
As they sweep along,
And I shout as loud as the loudest there;
And the sleepers awake,
Who fear and quake,
And can see to dress in the ruddy glare.
Hark, hark, to the mournful low of the cattle:
And list to the poultry's fearful scream:
I love the noise, the confusion, and rattle

Of crackling rafter and falling beam.
To stack and shed
The flames they spread;
I joy as the fire flakes upward fly:
And I love to hear
That no water is near,
And I grin with delight when the pumps are dry.
Oh, I love to see on every tree
The bright flames playing far and wide,
Making the darkness of night to flee,
And revealing the things that night would hide.
See, see, how they fall
On the old Church wall,
And gild the vane on the old grey tower;
And dance round the bed
Of the sleeping dead
You may read their names at the midnight hour.
Some love to read of murmering rills,
And shady lanes, and flowery vales,
And waving woods, and sunny hills:
To me there's no charm in such flimsy tales.
The volcano's frown,
And the burning town,
These, these are the themes that never tire:
And the auto de fe,
And the wild suttee,
And my very dreams are of smoke and fire.[27]

The Song of the Incendiary

John Stallon's way with fire had certainly brought the
'volcano's frown' to Rectory Farm, rattling the awkward peace
of Great Shelford, poised on the brink of Enclosure.

Once such excitement had been tasted, how could that taste
ever be lost?

Chapter Seven

THE MARK OF JOHN STALLON

He was not ignorant; for he had learned both to read and write.
Appendix, Funeral Sermon of John Stallon.

Sadly for us, no example of John Stallon's writing – if he ever produced any – remains. I realise there is just one possible trace of his way with letters in existence: his signature in the marriage registry from the church in Great Shelford.

I travel to the Cambridgeshire County Archives in Ely, pointed there by a note in the digital transcript of the parish records noting the original marriage register for St Mary the Virgin – on the which the digital record is based – is stored there.

The helpful people at the Archive apologise; they have no originals. Have I tried the parish church?

Back at Great Shelford, I cycle to meet the churchwarden, Bob Doel. As requested, I have brought with me a pair of hastily-purchased white cotton archivist's gloves – and also a face mask, for we are still in the times of Covid.

We enter the freezing cold rabbit hole of the vestry at St Mary the Virgin, like scrubbed-up surgeons, drawn by Tenniel.

In fact, Bob is a former churchwarden. Now retired, he is – like many a writer – fatally available for menial tasks during office hours. He has helpfully dug out the marriage register from the 1800s to aid my research.

Carefully turning the pages to 1820, I see the names of 'John Stallion' (Bachelor of this parish) and Elisabeth Patman (Single Woman of this parish), and their witnesses, John Hasell and William Elborne.

Perhaps John is anxious not to embarrass his illiterate

bride and workmates by signing his name, so flaunting his original superpower. Or perhaps the Reverend Henry Finch does not know his parishioners as well as he thinks he does. He assumes these labourers are illiterate and fills their names out – complete with a misspelling of John's last name – in advance of the service. Either way, John Stallon's name, and that of his bride, are marked only with a cross.

It is a powerful sign of John's approaching fate.

★

There is one reason Elizabeth is glad to stay home from the fields at harvest.

As well as being a time of high spirits, harvest is also a season of greater freedom for women. This has its positive side. Many of the girls Elizabeth grew up with found husbands in the warm evenings and remote hay ricks of the summer. Elizabeth by contrast, is viewed with fear or suspicion – and not just by older people with tales of crooked witches rattling around their heads. Before she was married, Elizabeth Patman would frequently find herself working alone – all the more so when her workmates got distracted by the prospect of a roll in the straw. Farmer's sons, or even farmers, aware of all the high living going on in the corners of their land, aroused by it, sometimes convinced themselves some convenient satisfaction was their due. And what was a lone woman – however bent and slow-moving – if not convenient?

Like most labouring women of the time – and many women in our own time – Elizabeth had a gallery of men's faces etched in her mind. In her case, they were men around the village, people to avoid – and perhaps take revenge on, should the opportunity arise.

For now, Elizabeth feels the weight of her new child dogging her movements from the inside, even as she cleans about the house. Hearing the alarm sounded this morning

for what she quickly learned was a fire at Rectory Farm –
she duly felt alarm herself. John would be in the thick of it
– fighting fire, breathing smoke, dodging exploding timbers
– and perhaps also dodging discovery. She has no room in her
heart today for anything but hope; a safe passage through the
day for herself and the baby, and deliverance for John, too.

She takes another sip of her ale and tells John Junior
sharply – too sharply – that No, he can't go out to help with
the engine. He must copy his letters as John has shown him.
His father will check them when he's home.

Chapter Eight

LORD HARDWICKE LENDS A HAND.

It is for the honour of our county, it is for our credit as men, that we must find out and punish these cowardly miscreants. Englishmen were never assassins! Englishmen were never incendiaries…

East Anglian Times, 23 November 1830

It is four days since the fire at Rectory Farm.

Three years from now Philip Yorke, 3rd Earl of Hardwicke will, like John Stallon, be dead. But today the Earl has been forced to drag himself, aged seventy-four, from one of his favourite occupations; studying the habits of the ichneumon wasp.

Parasitic wasps have their uses. They are known to inject their eggs into the larvae of an impressive range of pests from butterflies to beetles. Once hatched, the ichneumon's offspring ruthlessly destroy the host from the inside. Thus may pests be suppressed – and crop yields correspondingly boosted. For an agricultural improver like the Earl, this is not new knowledge. It has been known, in fact, for a hundred years and with this parasitic assistance, England might yet make a decent fist of feeding its people – if only the ichneumons would breed in captivity.

Still, duty calls, and there's an end to it.

The interruption to the Earl's studies comes this morning in the form of two men from the county, requesting his assistance. Yorke listens, as one must, and solemnly undertakes to give the matter his utmost consideration and more importantly, to act.

To emphasise the independence yet co-dependence of these elements – consideration, and action – has always, in the Earl's experience, played well with working people. It seems so in this case. As he walks his visitors out of the estate office of the great and beautiful house that is the county seat at Wimpole Hall, the farmers seem buoyed by the Earl's profession of support.

The trouble is, 'action' means Yorke's time with the ichneumons is over for the day; his duty lies in less calming pursuits. By the time the farmers have swung away down the Hall's long western approach, the Earl has already made a decision. He climbs the stone steps to re-enter the house by the grand main entrance.

There will follow another long climb up the main staircase of the house, and a march through the famous Yellow Drawing room to reach Yorke's private study, tucked away in the north-west corner of the building. The gout that has been his constant companion for more than thirty years – since he first strode the stage of national government as Lord Lieutenant of Ireland – is agony this morning. Now that he is alone, he can at least lean fully on the banister rail, hauling himself crab-like past the family daubings.

From flies to crabs. As the Earl progresses, he reflects that the inheritance of his earldom seems determined to progress in a similarly crab-like fashion from generation to generation. Just as he inherited the title from his uncle, Yorke knows the title, on his own death, will pass to *his* nephew. Yorke has in fact four perfectly adequate daughters, but all by dint of being female are barred from inheriting. His four sons on the other hand have all failed – each in his own sad way – to survive. Not something Philip himself can be accused of.

As a young man, Yorke had entered politics as an energetic Whig but was independently minded enough to spot the Tory William Pitt offered something else – something vital the country needed. Hence the job in Ireland. In that role – perhaps to Pitt's surprise, and despite clear royal opposition – Hardwicke supported the emancipation of the Catholic people of Ireland. Never let it be said that Philip Yorke kowtows to power.

Fortunately, given the gout, his six years as Lord Lieutenant of Ireland are long over. Philip remains however, Lord Lieutenant of his home county. As such he is obliged to intervene now and then in the lives of the people of Cambridgeshire. And this is very much a 'now' moment.

Reaching his study – sanctuary from his wife's scarlets and purples – Philip looks from his window at the coal-faced sheep mulching in the North Meadow, his Norfolk Horns. At the other, eastern extreme of the building, separated from the Hall by a matter of yards, stands the parish church of St Andrew. It is here the Earl has decided he will be buried. Pitt is no more, like each of Yorke's sons; one son died at one year of age, another at four, a third at thirteen, and the great hope – already an MP in his own right by the age of twenty-four – drowned at sea, shipwrecked in the Baltic. The nephew will consequently inherit. This particular nephew is also a Philip, as it happens, and a sailor, like the Earl's beloved son. Rumour has it the proto-Fourth Earl is about to marry; the timing of Yorke's posthumous relocation will be good when it comes.

Good God man! Hardwicke shakes these morbid thoughts from his head. He must write a letter to his old collaborator, Viscount Melbourne at the Home Office, and see if he can stir some action. The farmers' intelligence suggests malcontents are again setting fire to the county, and everything that has been tried thus far has proved damnably ephemeral. Not two years ago, three Cambridgeshire labourers were hanged for arson in the city – supposedly as an object lesson. And here we are again. Yorke finds he is losing the taste for inflicting mortality for moral ends. Perhaps it is time to appeal to an even baser instinct in his fellow men. Money.

Philip Yorke – still the 3rd Earl last time he looked – lowers himself into his favourite upright chair and reaches forward for paper. He finds his pen, takes ink from the inkwell, and settles again into the shell of a man of significance. A moment's thought, and his hand begins its own crab-like journey across the page.

The letter he writes, which I retrieve from the National Archive at Kew, is in parts, utterly undecipherable:

Private Wimpole December 19, 1831.

My dear Lord,

In consequence of a fire which took place on Thursday last in Great Shelford, about five miles from Cambridge, two farmers in an adjoining parish, who are also [proprietors?] of [lands?], have just applied to me for the purpose of [enquiring?] wheth– whether [sic] it is likely [that?] upon a proper [representation?] of the case, any reward for the discovery of the offender would be offered by Government.

I told them I believed it was not the [practise?] of Government to offer rewards for the discovery of offenders; but that [it?] [frequently?] happened in cases that [unclear] rewards are offered by [such?] [including?] [when?] a promise of the King's pardon was at [the?] same time [offered?] to persons giving such information as would [convict?] the offender [unclear].

Since hearing their questions [there?] has been no [unclear] and thus I have undertaken to [procure?] information upon the [subject ?]

I request your Lordship will [unclear] inform me whether in any cases of this [nature?] rewards are offered by Government.

The Farm where this conflagration took place is the property of Jesus College, and the Tenant holds the tythes of the [Parish?] under that [Society?] [unclear] no conjecture can be formed as to the incendiary, or the cause that might have led to the crime.

The Tenant Mr Headley[sic] is insured with Sun Fire office office (sic) to the full amount of his loss, so that the only sufferers by the Fire, will be the labourers of the Parish, who will be deprived of the employment of threshing and a [lost?] [share?] of the corn, which has been consumed in the barns and stacks of the Farmer.

A meeting of the magistrates was held on Saturday in Cambridge, but I am sorry to say no v [sic] satisfactory information was obtained

as to the origin of the fire.
I have the honour to remain, with great [unclear], my Dear Lord.
Your faithful
and obedient servant,
Hardwicke
[The?] [Right?] [Honourable?]
[Viscount?] Melbourne
[Unclear] [unclear] [unclear] [28]

Who were these 'two farmers' who lobbied Hardwicke so effectively? The Earl's letter does not say, and I can find no other account of the meeting.

Smart money has to be on two men in particular. Henry Headly, the most recent victim of the incendiaries, is an obvious candidate. The other is his near neighbour, a man called Peter Grain. These men, in fact, constitute one half of a ruling elite in Great Shelford. The more papers I wade through in the archive, the more I come to think of these operators as Great Shelford's 'Big Four'.

Most villages in rural England at the time had a Lord of the Manor (sometimes more than one) who derived their status from the Crown. Support at times of trial, and mediation in matters of dispute – these are roles villagers might expect to be played by their Lord of the Manor. South Cambridgeshire is unusual in this respect. Most of its land is owned not by the Crown but by Cambridge University Colleges. In Great Shelford, Gonville & Caius College, Jesus College, and St John's College own almost every blade of grass.

Because they are interested almost entirely in the receipt of rents, the colleges generally behave like absentee landlords, leasing their Manors (and their surrounding demesnes) to wealthy farmers. In this situation it is these 'tenants', the biggest farmers in the village, who both carry the burden for their fellow villagers' welfare and determine what happens in village matters. Time and again in the first third of the

nineteenth century, four names recur in prosecuting the
affairs of Great Shelford: Henry Headly, his brother William
Headly, Thomas Stacey (farmer and churchwarden), and most
prominently of all, Peter Grain. The last owns, or occupies as
a tenant of the colleges, more than a third of the entire land
in the village – and more in the villages beyond.

Lord Melbourne's private secretary, a man called I.M.
Phillips, doesn't have time to speculate on the identity of
these lobbyists. His expertise lies in sucking the marrow from
any communication the Home Secretary receives. Hacking
through the post, the morning after Lord Hardwicke penned
his illegible letter, Phillips screws up his eyes just as I have
done and somehow deciphers the scrawl before him. He
notes the essentials in pencil on the cover.

> *Wimpole Dec 19 1831*
> *Lord Hardwicke*
> *fire at Great Shelford about five miles from Cambridge.*
> *are rewards offered by Government in cases of This Nature.*

Phillips' most crucial note follows when the letter returns
from Viscount Melbourne's desk. It is written in pencil:

> *Reward and pardon offered.*

Within days, a striking advertisement appears in the pages
of the *Cambridge Chronicle,* with the following headline:

Eight Hundred Pounds Reward and Pardon

Whitehall December 22nd 1831.
*Whereas it hath been humbly represented unto the King, that the fire
discovered upon the property of Mr. Henry Headly, on the fifteenth day of
December, and that it is strongly suspected the above premises were wilfully and
maliciously set on fire by some evil-disposed person or persons unknown. His
Majesty, for the better apprehending and bringing to justice the offender before*

mentioned, is hereby pleased to promise His most gracious PARDON and a reward of FOUR HUNDRED POUNDS to anyone of them (except the person who actually set fire to the said premises) giving such information as shall lead to the apprehension and conviction of the said offender or offenders.

Henry Headly and Peter Grain – and come to that, Lord Hardwicke – are that rarest breed of men: people who have got action from government when they needed it. But the four hundred pounds promised by the King (or by Melbourne on his behalf) is only half the story. The advertisement continues:

And as further encouragement an additional REWARD of FOUR HUNDRED POUNDS is hereby offered. Such last mentioned reward to be paid upon application to Messrs. Nash and Wedd, Solicitors, Royston.[29]

Hmmm.

Messrs Nash and Wedd (solicitors) of Royston have as far as I can tell no direct link with Great Shelford – apart from the daily stagecoach that passes through both those settlements, part of a five-and-half-hour rattle from London to Cambridge. But Nash and Wedd's articled clerk in 1831 is a man called Henry Thurnall. Thurnall and his family live in the village of Whittlesford – like Shelford, counted in the Thriplow Hundred, and just a few miles from Great Shelford itself.

In fact, Messrs Nash and Wedd (solicitors) were on Thurnall's account recently caught up in a catastrophe threatening to envelop the entire village of Whittlesford. This is how it began: three village labourers – Ephraim Lichfield, John Nunn the elder and Simeon Nunn the younger – chose one night to set upon, rob, and badly beat a man driving his gig in the lanes of Whittlesford after dark. Their victim was Henry Thurnall, the clerk at Nash & Wedd, returning from his work at the office in Royston. The assailants claimed they did not recognise it was their fellow villager they were so violently assaulting. Towards Mr Thurnall they bore no ill feeling at all. Mr Thurnall however, did recognise them. Ephraim, John and Simeon were swiftly arrested, tried – and sentenced to death for their crime.

Appalled that such a disaster should befall the village for his sake, Henry Thurnall hastily consulted his employers. They quickly organised a petition for clemency. Again held in the National Archive at Kew, this plea has a typically legal-sounding premise: if criminals are executed for crimes which involve no loss of life, then surely others ne'er do-wells tempted into similar crimes will be persuaded to finish the job by leaving no one alive to identify their attackers. The effect of this capital sentence would thus be the very opposite of the deterrence it was intended to achieve.

The petition was circulated in the village and garnered the signatures of eight worthy citizens of Whittlesford including the 'prosecutor' or victim, Henry Thurnall – and also the vicar of the parish.[30]

Alas, Messrs Wedd and Nash (and Thurnall) had expended their powers of reasoning in vain. Lord Melbourne – like many a Home Secretary before and since – was determined to stamp hard on perpetrators of violence. He refused all pleas for clemency. The men were scheduled to be hanged, and that was that. And then came a U-turn. The Home Office exercised mercy – of a typically nineteenth century kind. The sentences of the older men were commuted to penal servitude for the remainder of their lives. The younger Nunn, Simeon, was transported to Australia, with a slim chance of ever seeing his village or loved ones again.

And now, even as this very mixed salvation for his own village worked itself out, Henry Thurnall – and the older men who own the solicitors practise where he works – find themselves agents for an additional sum of four hundred pounds, matching that of the Crown, as a reward in the case of the Shelford arsonist. They have the opportunity to help find this perpetrator, and so nip this latest outbreak of rural brutishness in the bud.

An intriguing question enters my head; who puts up this generous additional bounty? Possibly, it is the solicitors themselves. They each have possible motive, and together, they have the means.

Mr Wedd, the senior partner had been appointed to the office of 'Attorney to the Court of the Exchequer' only one month earlier; four hundred pounds might seem a small price for the chance to demonstrate how well Mr Wedd can walk in step with the King.[31] For Henry Thurnall, the articled clerk, it is more likely a moral question. His faith in the goodness of men and women has been shaken by the attack on him – and here is an opportunity for Great Shelford to demonstrate virtue, purging itself of its arsonist before harm comes to another fellow human. For Mr Nash, Henry Thurnall represents a ready-made replacement for his aging partner – someone who can take on the bulk of the more energetic work in the practise. Let young Henry have his largesse as some men have their sport. For Nash and Wedd (later to become Nash, Wedd and Thurnall, and later still just Nash & Thurnall) four hundred pounds could prove money well spent.

As you are reading this, you should dismiss from your thoughts the notion that £400 of the King's money plus £400 from Nash and Wedd, makes eight hundred pounds. Today, that would barely buy a minibreak. £68,000 on the other hand (or £88,000 in some estimates), could change a life. And for what? How much work is it for a man or woman, hands scarred from wielding a hoe or sickle, to whisper a name in a magistrate's ear? Or, if they have their letters – which most don't – to write that name down on a scrap of paper filched from the paper mill in Sawston? Little, you might think. But loosing tongues among working men and women in rural Cambridgeshire at this time is what the locals call, strong work. There are many among the poorer sort who feel themselves engaged in a long war of attrition with their employers. They are determined to keep their lips sealed.

Still, someone must have put the money up. If it is not the solicitors themselves, other candidates are the Earl himself, or Peter Grain – whether in concert with fellow members of the 'Big Four', or alone. He, like the Earl, like the solicitors, certainly has the means.

Perhaps a more important question than the source of this extra incentive is: who takes the next step in tackling the scourge of incendiarism – and on whose recommendation? The answer to the last is that it is probably Melbourne's secretary, I.M. Phillips, who suggests – to the Earl? The Big Four? Peter Grain alone? – that professional help is needed in detecting the culprit or culprits behind the fire at Rectory Farm.

Whatever the case, a request is made to the Bow Street Public Office in London to send an experienced detective to the village without delay. It is just such an experienced officer – a so-called Bow Street Runner – who accepts the call and travels to Great Shelford by the next available stagecoach.

Thanks to the Earl of Hardwicke's reluctant neglect of his parasitic wasps, the hunt for the Shelford arsonist – like the campaign of fire-raising itself – has just accelerated. John Stallon does not know it yet, but his incendiarism has lit a very long fuse.

Chapter Nine

THE TRIUMPHS OF HERCULES

Shelford Ca. [*Scelford* c1050 KCD 907, -a c1080 ICC, *Escelforde* DB, *Scheldford* 1190 P, *Shelford parva* 1228 FF, Schelford Magna 1254 Val] S~Nt [Scelforde DB, Sceldford c DC, Scelford 1232 CH, *Scheldford Magna* 1276 Ipm]. The first el. may be OE *sceld* in the sense 'shelter' (cf. SHELDWICH) or an OE **sceldu* 'shallowness, shallow place'.

The Concise Oxford Dictionary of English Place Names

A coach called *The Beehive* picks up its passengers from just behind the *Three Nuns Inn,* Aldgate, London, at 4.30pm every Tuesday, Thursday and Saturday – returning from Cambridge at 10am on the alternate days. After leaving the *Nuns,* the Northbound coach makes a brief stop at *The Catherine Wheel* in Bishopsgate Street, takes on fresh horses at *The Bull* in Royston, and finally charges into Cambridge five or six bone-shattering hours later. There it disgorges its contents, groggy from the ordeal.[32] This, in late December 1831, is how those who can afford it, suffer for their travel. Those whose business is more urgent, take the mail coach.

The Boston Mail is the coach in question; with its daily mound of correspondence secured under armed guard, the coach in addition carries a maximum of four paying customers. Thus loaded, the *Boston* hurtles out of the capital every day on the stroke of midnight. After a swift change of horses in the Cambridgeshire village of Melbourne it arrives at the post office at 24 Green Street, central Cambridge, in a total journey time of just four and a half hours.[33]

On the morning of December 31st 1831, one passenger at

least emerges bright-eyed and full of resolution. This man has flown to Cambridge (if that's the word) to consult with local magistrates on a matter of the utmost importance.

Important or not, arriving before 5am necessitates a hearty breakfast. The *Red Lion* in the narrow lane of Petty Cury will doubtless oblige.

Annoyingly, it is turned midday before a meeting with the magistrates can be joined. Once met, the two parties exchange letters. In the stranger's case, these comprise a few words of introduction and a warrant for the arrest of the Shelford Arsonist issued by Sir Richard Birnie, Chief Magistrate at the Bow Street Public Office. In return, the magistrates pledge to pay the stranger – now confirmed as a Principal Officer glorying in the name of Samuel Hercules Taunton – his 'reasonable expenses'. There is no mention at this point that Taunton is also due a share of the royal reward. That is taken for granted. This is how all Principal Officers make their living, a significant fillip to the modest retainer – £1.5s per week in 1832 – paid out by the Bow Street Office to all its officers, meticulously, each quarter.

After a brief consultation about the case, Taunton hails a fly-cab to speed him on to Great Shelford. He has never visited the village before but has been informed – or is it warned? – by the magistrates what to expect: Great Shelford is a medium-sized, 'not especially friendly' village, about five miles from Cambridge.

As the fly exhausts the city's streets the driver slows to negotiate the rougher road surface slicing its way between the open fields of Trumpington. Taunton is conscious that a copy of the *Cambridge Chronicle* announcing the Crown's intervention in the matter lies folded at the bottom of his travelling case. Even a detective as confident as Samuel Hercules Taunton finds comfort, knowing the reward – in print at least – is already in the bag.

★

In addition to the business of finance, there are a few other things it is useful to know about the corps of Principal Officers at Bow Street – the crack squad from which Taunton has been drawn.

This elite band of detectives was established by none other than the novelist Henry Fielding, in 1748/9. Fielding was of course, acting in his other capacity – that of Justice of the Peace for Westminster. The service remained in existence until 1839 when it was absorbed into the Metropolitan Police Service, established in 1829. In the ninety years it was operating independently, the squad's numbers rarely rose to more than eight officers, and never more than twelve. To join the corps, a candidate must wait for an existing officer to retire, to change professions, or die. [34]

Samuel Taunton has been a Principal Officer for almost twenty years when he arrives in Shelford, amassing considerable experience. Conversant in French, his cases 'out of town' sometimes involve travels to Europe to question a witness, say, or to arrest a suspect. But his life has not always been so exciting. Prior to promotion, Taunton was a constable in the foot patrol, also based at Bow Street.[35] Samuel Taunton is that rare thing – a person of culture who is also familiar with the rougher ways of the world. Like all Bow Street officers, he knows how to survive.

PF Hetherington, whose *Chronicles of the Bow Street Police-Office* offered one of the first histories of the Principal Officer adds, in 1888, that the Bow Street Runners – a popular nickname that Officers like Taunton professed to hate, but we might suspect, actually quite enjoyed – could easily be distinguished in any crowded street by their bright red waistcoats.[36]

True, it is hard to imagine Samuel Hercules Taunton

(SHT) without a waistcoat, probably quite a fancy one, for as we shall see, he is a man not only of energy but of a certain theatrical bent. His dress for a 'country case' however is more likely to have been modelled on that established by his fellow officer, William Salmon, in 1820.

Called to investigate a series of robberies plaguing the Suffolk wool town of Hadleigh in 1820, Salmon *'assumed the dress of a labouring man, and visited at night the public houses where suspicious characters were in the habit of resorting'*.

At one of these pubs, the undercover Salmon observed four *'ill-looking men drinking together, who repeatedly looked at the clock; at the hour of ten one said "it is time to go", when they departed.'*

The next day it was discovered that a nearby watermill had been broken into – and a large quantity of flour and grain had been stolen. The four 'ill-looking men' were swiftly sought out and arrested.[37]

This kind of undercover work was still being practiced by Principal Officers attending 'country duties', ten years later. In 1830 – the time of the Swing Riots – Taunton and a number of his fellow officers were deployed to various parts of Southern England. Their goal was to gather intelligence on groups of potential rioters – and incendiaries. One of these Officers, Daniel Bishop, reported to the Home Office from Deal in Kent:

I have gone to the different Pot Houses in the Villages, disguised among the Labourers, of an evening and all their talk is about the wages...[38]

In the case that SHT is about to investigate, a major crime has already been committed. Mr Headly's barns at Rectory Farm are reduced to *'a heap of ruins'* as the *Globe* newspaper put it.[39] Like officer Salmon's robbery case at Hadleigh, this gross act of vandalism is not a single, one-off case; there have as we know been at least two earlier fires in Great Shelford within the last three years. The supposition must be it is the work of a serial offender – or offenders. The fact these offenders are yet to be detected demonstrates that once again Samuel Taunton faces cunning and careful adversaries.

★

Taunton is set down from the fly outside *The George and Dragon Inn* in Great Shelford. This ancient inn stands on the ribbon of road that runs past the church of St Mary the Virgin before crossing the river linking Shelford's Great and Little – and is bang next to Rectory Farm, squeezed between Headly's yard and the church. In the eighteen days since the fire, the yard has been cleaned up – Henry Headly is not a man to let the grass grow under his feet, let alone a pile of smouldering ash. The drooping roof of the Inn – still known locally almost two centuries later as a private house called 'Old Thatch' – is for now, safe. According to the cab driver, *The George* is the best inn the village can offer. For some years to come, it may be one of only two inns, the other being the Black Swan aka 'The Dirty Duck'. Smaller ale houses are though already beginning to sprout. Soon these will be joined by, or will morph into, popular pubs like *The Peacock, The Red Lion* and many more, the names and premises rising and sinking in a never-ending fluctuation of Cambridgeshire hospitality.

Taunton's first priority is to speak to Farmer Headly, to garner the farmer's own suspicions about the culprit. When eventually he finds him, this proves none too enlightening; Henry Headly finds it impossible to believe a local person could be responsible. It must be someone from outside – if not, he adds darkly, the agent of a foreign power.

Taunton thanks Mr Headly for his insights and returns to *The George*. Opening his travelling case, he stares at the work clothes he has brought with him – clothes that, following the example of officers Salmon and Bishop, would give him all the colourful plumage of a dunnock. He decides on a different strategy. First he will eat a light supper, and then his work will begin.

★

Church Street is already murky when Taunton emerges from the *George*. He is wearing his usual city clothes and city shoes, heading out to a beer house called *The Plough* which squats at the other end of the High Street, a few minutes distant. This, he has been told, is where the poorest labourers drink.

On entry, it is immediately clear to Taunton that if this is a 'home from home', then the lives of labourers in Great Shelford are poor indeed. Besides the barkeeper and himself (the only customer), there is an enormous keg of beer, a number of stools, and one chair. As Taunton enters, the barkeep weighs him for a moment, as if trying to decide whether this traveller is likely to stay long enough to warrant lighting a fire. The man orders a tankard, and so the barman's hand is forced. He puts a spark to the kindling in the old way, with his tinder box, and the grim coldness of the cottage-come-bar slowly, very slowly, transforms.

It takes a good half hour of careful and, in Taunton's case, non-committal pleasantries, before the detective/travelling wholesaler manages to steer his conversation with the barkeep round to the recent calamity at Rectory Farm. Frustratingly, he has only just done so when the arrival of another customer interrupts their conversation.

At first, the newcomer, like the barman before him, stands stock still when he sees Taunton. Had this encounter taken place in one of London's drinking holes, in the streets of Cheapside or Clerkenwell where SHT is well known, he might have taken this for a sign of guilt. But a detective must be a student of human behaviour; SHT knows that for a country person, the sight of a stranger, particularly one from the city, can be a shock. Indeed, that is part of his intended effect.

The local man is tall and gaunt-looking. He is not in the first flush of youth but can't be much more than half Taunton's sixty-three years. In the end, the man merely nods in the Taunton's direction, and then in the barman's, and is soon drawing on the same brackish liquid that Taunton himself must somehow consume.

Even allowing for the fact this is not whisky, there is something wrong about this ale. As Taunton lifts the tankard to his lips he is assailed by the smell of something odd. Odd, but familiar. For a time, the officer cannot place it. The ale has the same chastening bitterness on the back of the tongue as beer everywhere in England, but the smell is even more off-putting than usual. Finally, he has it. Some years ago, in a Belgian port city, the English Officer was offered a taste of something called a *banane*. Taunton knows this exotic fruit cannot be an ingredient of the beer, but the smell is unmistakeable – a bi-product of over-fast fermentation. It is not only the ale house that is new, Taunton concludes, but the brewer to his trade. Clearly, working people here are as adaptable and keen to improve themselves as anyone in the city – just less good at it.

By the time Taunton returns from his reverie in Antwerp, the youngish man is already draining his beer. The officer manages at least to establish that the fellow is one of Headly's men, and that Henry Headly, still a bachelor at more than sixty years of age, is well thought of in the village – a good employer. Wages are down, but 'Mr Headly pays what he

can,' the young man avers without prompting, and adds that
Henry Headly can have no enemy on god's earth. Asking the
younger man for his own opinion on the fire, Taunton finds
the poor fellow is capable of no independent thought at all.
He can only repeat his master's suspicions about outsiders.
At this point, the barman breaks into their conversation to
embarrass his established customer.

'This is one of the heroes who put out the fire', he informs
Taunton.

The worker drops his head in modesty.

'His wife is in the family way too', adds the barman,
clapping him on the shoulder, 'Stallion by name, Stallion by
nature. Can't be long now, eh John?'

Again, the younger man smiles awkwardly, and Taunton is
reminded what a strange mixture the rural man is; tough and
resilient, potentially violent – and also shy.

'I must get back', says John Stallon, and drains his tankard.
By the door he adds, 'It was a good thing no one 'ent killed
at this fire, Mr…?'

'Taunton', says the detective. 'Actually, it is Principal Officer
Taunton, from the Bow Street Public Office'.

'Ah' says his interlocuter, and nods, showing just the right
amount of surprise. 'Then I must wish you well with your
work. Our Masters will feel safer for it.'

As young Stallon pulls the door closed behind him, Officer
Taunton looks back to the fire, and reflects how rare it is for a
man, truly, to have no enemies. There will be someone in the
village who has it in for Henry Headly, the bachelor farmer,
and Taunton intends to find out who. It's as good a start as any.
He also ponders how impossible it is to enter a small village
as a stranger without being noticed, whatever your disguise –
and whatever the likes of William Salmon and Daniel Bishop
tell themselves. At least now Great Shelford will know the law
is urgently on the trail of the criminal amongst them – and

that might shake something from the tree.

SHT sits before the fire for some time after that, reflecting too on the impossible quantity of god-awful country ale still swilling about in the bottom of his tankard.

★

Despite the disappointments we have attributed to Taunton's night at the *Plough*, Samuel Hercules Taunton loses no time in flushing a suspect into the open. By January the second, the *Cambridge Chronicle* is reporting that officer Taunton has already collared his man. Joseph Ellerm (or Ellum) is a pauper – a poor labourer fallen on even harder times than Farmer Headly's employees. In exchange for money from the parish to buy food, Ellerm had been set to work in a gravel pit close by Rectory Farm on the very morning that the fire broke out. He is, in Taunton's estimation, the epitome of a malcontent. He was also seen loitering around the churchyard that lies just the other side of *The George & Dragon*, and thus, just a stone's throw – or a fiery brand's heave – from the fated barns.

In the case of officer Salmon's Hadleigh mill-raid, back in 1820, once an arrest was made, Salmon the Bow Street Runner had behaved in a manner astonishingly like the desperate detective of a modern crime procedural. According to the newspaper account mentioned above, the four suspects were '*placed in separate rooms with men to watch over them, in the course of the next night, one of them…confessed the whole transaction.*' The confessor is then persuaded to turn witness for the Crown and his confederates are promptly committed for trial. Case closed.

Once Ellerm is arrested, Officer Taunton's methods prove in comparison, even more crude. Dangerous though it may be to judge a nineteenth century case by modern standards, SHT's 'method' is familiar not so much from a routine crime drama, but from several contemporary miscarriages of justice.

A likely suspect, or suspects – frequently someone with a degree of vulnerability – is arrested. There then follow hours of intensive questioning, the detective intent on breaking the prisoner down, forcing a confession and so wrapping up the case.

To be fair to Samuel Taunton, in the 1830s forensic science is still a dream. A confession – however obtained – is easily the best means of wringing a conviction from any jury. And Taunton has also discovered a witness, prepared to say that Ellerm had previously been overheard wishing that Headly's farm was a pile of ashes.

But Joseph Ellerm is certainly vulnerable. That much is clear from *The Globe*'s account of the interaction between Taunton and the prisoner on the day of his arrest:

> *The prisoner is described as a grossly illiterate man, and so ignorant of the consequences of the crime with which he is charged, that in conversation with the officer, he was under an impression that an imprisonment of six months was the only punishment which could be inflicted on a party found guilty of such an offence.*[40]

The term *grossly illiterate* is telling. It is still part of a grim pattern of criminal prosecution more than a century later. In 1976 a twenty-four year-old West Yorkshire man called Stefan Kiszko was convicted of the rape and murder of an 11 year-old girl. The evidence against Kiszko was minimal, but Stefan had the mental age of a seven-year-old. Fatefully, his hobby was collecting car number plates. One of the numbers in his notebook was that of a car known to have been in the area where the hideous attack took place – which put Stefan at the scene of the crime. Not much you might think, to hang a case on, but four young girls had complained that Kiszko had exposed himself to them the day before the murder. (They later admitted they had made this claim up, 'for a laugh').

After three days of intensive questioning, Kiszko – deprived of a solicitor and denied also the presence of his mother – confessed to all the charges against him. Kiszko spent the next sixteen years in prison, before a campaign and appeal established his innocence and finally secured his released. Barely a year later, his broken health led to heart failure, and Stefan Kiszko died.[41]

Kiszko's case, and those like it, should be a lesson, but in 1991 another vulnerable man was accused of murdering a London shopkeeper, Baldev Hoondle. Oliver Campbell was convicted, like Kiszko, largely on the basis of a confession. The life sentence Campbell received – and for which he served eleven years in prison – was commuted to a life licence only when, once again, supporters launched an appeal. Campbell had long maintained his innocence, saying his confession was extracted during the eleventh of fourteen police interviews that followed his arrest. The pressure exerted by police in those interviews was described by Campbell as 'relentless'.

In fact, Campbell had sustained brain damage at birth, resulting in severe learning difficulties and an IQ of 73. Despite being aware of this, the social work support present in the first ten of his interviews was not made available in the succeeding four. He did though, in the eyes of his accusers, fit the bill; he was black, more than six feet tall, and heavily built. In total, Oliver Campbell waited thirty-four years before being acquitted, his conviction finally quashed in 2024. In the early nineteenth century even this measure of justice would have come way too late.[42]

After his arrest by Samuel Taunton on Monday the second of January 1832, Joseph Ellerm's own nightmare was just beginning. First, he found himself imprisoned in the County Gaol at Cambridge Castle. There he was repeatedly questioned by the smartly-dressed man from London.

Sometimes the newspapers mention a magistrate being present, sometimes not. To his credit, Ellerm refused to admit any guilt, but this did not stop him being questioned again the following Saturday and then being committed for trial at the forthcoming Lent Assizes.

Was SHT confident he had the right man? Did he, in good faith, believe he had enough evidence to secure a conviction? Apparently so, for the *Northampton Mercury* reports on Saturday 14th of January, another dramatic development:

'At Bow Street on Thursday night, just before Sir R. Birnie left the bench, Taunton the officer reported to the magistrates that he had just returned from Cambridgeshire, where he had been assisting in the investigation of an atrocious case of arson at Great Shelford, a village five miles from Cambridge. Early in the morning of the 15th December, two barns filled with corn, some stables, and some farming implements to the amount of £2,000, were set on fire, and totally destroyed. These were the property of a farmer named Headley, who had been totally ruined by the occurrence.'

Leaving aside Taunton's failure to mention the small – and merciful – matter of Headly's insurance cover, and the prisoner's continued denials of guilt, the officer's pivotal role is made abundantly clear – if not the correct name of the 'offender':

'He (Taunton) had succeeded in tracing the commission of the offence so completely to a pauper named James Ellum, that on Weds 4th instant, he was fully committed for trial at the next Cambridge assizes. The above is the third fire which has taken place within a comparatively short period in the neighbourhood of Great Shelford'.

Much of the 'sexing up' of facts we might detect here may be down to the 'flair' of the reporter. But there is no doubt Taunton is keen to make an impact on his Bow Street audience – and not least on Justice Birnie himself. Two years earlier Birnie had publicly torn the officer off a strip for making an arrest without first securing a warrant.[43] 'Now look at me', Taunton seems to be saying, 'no such problem this time'.

A conclusion to the case, and a share of the reward, are tantalisingly close.

Joseph Ellerm's reward meanwhile is several weeks shut up in Robert Orridge's prison in Cambridge Castle awaiting trial for arson – a crime that, contrary to Joseph's earlier guesses, carries a capital sentence. From his tiny cell in the gaol, Joseph cannot see the gallows; they are a temporary affair, erected each time that hangings are due. Yet somehow, for reasons Joseph cannot unravel, the gibbet's shadow is falling across him. The end of his small and troubled life seems suddenly, and terrifyingly, close.

Chapter Ten

THE TRIUMPHS OF HERCULES II

Mene, mene, tekel, parsin.
You have been weighed on the scales and found wanting.
The Book of Daniel, chapter 5, v27.

Quite how Officer Taunton felt when he learned which judge would be sitting at the Lent Assizes in Cambridge in 1832, we can't tell. Probably, he was excited, for the judge's name was Baron Gurney.

The paths of the two men had crossed some twelve years earlier, in a case that grabbed the attention of the nation and made the reputations of both men. The two had, in that very famous case, collaborated magnificently in pursuit of justice.

Judge Baron Gurney was then plain Mr John Gurney, prosecuting counsel in one of the most sensational cases the British courts had ever entertained. A total of twelve men were charged with plotting to murder the entire British Cabinet, including the Prime Minister, Lord Liverpool. Two of the gang's number were soon persuaded to incriminate the rest. The remaining ten stood trial for treason at the Old Bailey in April 1820. The case would become known as the Cato Street Conspiracy.

The men had been arrested in a huge police operation in which Samuel Taunton and all his fellow Bow Street Runners had participated, under the direction of their JP, Sir James Birnie. Deciding not to wait for the arrival of their pre-arranged back-up – in the form of the Coldstream Guards – the Runners moved in to arrest the conspirators. Two officers, George Ruthven and Richard Smithers were sent to Cato Street, just off the Edgware Road, where the ringleaders were meeting to finalise their plans. Richard Smithers (a member of the foot patrol), was killed in the brawl that ensued, run-through with a sword. The other officers simultaneously raided other addresses around London. Taunton and his partner were directed to arrest two of the gang – John (also known as James) Brunt and Richard Tidd – in the boarding house where they were staying, kept by a lady called Mary Rogers. There they also recovered a huge cache of weapons and explosives with which the outrage was allegedly to have been perpetrated.[44]

When the case came to court, Mr Gurney prosecuted for the Crown. SHT was not only a key witness for the prosecution but played a key role in the dramatic revelations Gurney laid out before the jury.

Taunton was not called to give his evidence until very close to the end of proceedings on the first day, the main stuff of which was the trial of the two defendants in whose arrest he had been involved, Brunt and Tidd. The exchange between Crown and Witness is recorded like this:

You are an officer of Bow-street?
Yes, I am.
On the morning of Thursday 24th of February, did you go to the lodgings of the prisoner Brunt?
I did.
Did you apprehend him?
I did.
At about what hour?
Between seven and eight in the morning.
What room did you find him in?
In a front two pair of stairs room.
You had, I suppose, another officer with you?
There was.
Did you leave him in the front room in custody of that officer, and go and search the back room two pair of stairs.

Yes I did.

I need not take the enumeration of that now, but did you find a quantity of fire-balls, grenades, gunpowder and other things?

I did.

In two baskets?

In two baskets.

[...]

Did you then proceed to the lodging of Tidd?

I did so.

Did you find some more grenades, and cartridges, and bullets?

I did.

Mr Gurney then apparently addresses the judge;

That is all I propose to ask him at present, the enumeration we need not go through twice...[45]

The Judge agrees, and moments later, the proceedings are adjourned till the next day. Having planted the thought of those two baskets, and all those explosives in the minds of the jury before they sleep, Gurney is content to pick up the matter the next day:

Samuel Hercules Taunton, called again.
Examined by Mr. Gurney.

You mentioned yesterday, that upon searching the two-pair back room in the house in which Brunt lodged, you found two rush baskets?

Yes.

Produce those two baskets?

These are the two baskets (Producing them).

What does that basket contain?

Nine different papers of tar, rope-yarn, and things of that description.

Are they what you call fire-balls?

They are.[....]

What have you in that basket? (my emphasis)

There are four grenades three papers of rope-yarn, tar, and more ingredients, two bags of gunpowder, of one pound each.

Produce those bags of gunpowder?

These are they; and five empty bags, a paper of powder, one leathern bag with sixty-three balls in it (producing them).[46]

Taunton goes on to repeat this rabbit-from-a-hat routine, producing the arsenal found at the lodgings of the other defendant, Tidd. This includes 434 bullets, 171 ball cartridges, 69 ball-cartridges without powder, a brown paper parcel with three pounds of gunpowder, ten grenades fitted with fuses, eleven one-pound bags of gunpowder, more bullets, flints and 965 more ball cartridges in parcels of five.

The trials of all the accused in the Cato Street case took a full twelve days to complete and proceeded in a similar manner. Not surprisingly, faced with overwhelming evidence revealed in this powerfully dramatic way, the jury found all the accused guilty. All were given the most extreme sentence for treason allowed by the law; they were to be publicly hanged, drawn and quartered.

In the event, that familiar nineteenth century mercy was extended to the accused. Five of the men were transported to Australia for life, and five – Brunt, Tidd, Thistlewood, Ings and Davidson, the only black defendant – were simply hanged in the normal way, and then decapitated.

The drama of these executions certainly overshadows all the drama of the court procedure that went before. Still, as he returned to Cambridge for the Lent Assizes ahead of the trial of Joseph Ellerm, SHT must surely have felt confident. He had been found dependable and useful to Mr – now Baron Gurney – in this previous, and momentous judicial encounter. Moreover, in the intervening years Gurney had established a reputation as a hard judge, resolutely applying the full force of the law. In another notorious case, he would insist on the death penalty for two men named James Pratt and John Smith found guilty of sodomy – on very slender evidence – because that was what the law required for such a conviction. Baron Gurney thus became the last judge in England to deliver a capital sentence for the 'crime' of performing a homosexual act. [47] He was also a swift dispenser of justice; referred to by one less than admiring colleague on the bench as tearing through his cases 'like a wild elephant charging through a sugar cane plantation'. [48] Taunton had good reason to believe the case would go his way.

Gurney was though, also known – sodomy cases apart – as a stickler for evidence.

There is, sadly, no surviving transcript of the case against Joseph Ellerm when it reached the Cambridge Assizes on March 16, 1832, so we have no idea of the evidence Taunton had amassed. Nor can we judge the power of any witness testimony he might have been planning to call. We can't even know whether the 'prosecutor' or victim, Henry Headly, still had any appetite for the case; the farmer would by now be in receipt of his very ample insurance pay-out, while Ellerm, dependent on the parish, probably seemed very poor prey. None of that can be known for sure, for one very good reason. Relayed by the newspapers and recorded in beautiful script in the court's Minute Book are three simple words: No True Bill. [49]

Joseph Ellerm had, in Baron Gurney's judgement and that of the Grand Jury, no case to answer. Taunton's evidence was simply insufficient to warrant continuing with a prosecution. This, despite poor Joe Ellerm having been imprisoned without trial or recompense for almost two months. This was a point not lost on the less establishment-minded court scribblers. The *Morning Herald's* correspondent of March 16, 1832 pointed out that it was hardly an isolated incident where arson was concerned:

...there were no less than four commitments for this crime in the calendar at the Cambridge Assizes, in <u>every case</u> of which an intelligent and considerate Grand Jury found it their duty to <u>throw out the Bill</u>. In two of these cases the individuals, against whom this charge had been brought, for which there was not a shadow of proof, had been in custody <u>five months</u>!

In another case the term of imprisonment was one month, and in the fourth instance, four months. What a state things have come to, in this once great and flourishing country, that British subjects can be for such long periods deprived of their liberty, and treated as felons, although the charge against them is so groundless that a Grand Jury cannot even find a bill! Yet, if these four men, or any of them, had been convicted upon evidence ever so slight, we have reason to think, from what have seen, that they would have been <u>executed</u>.

Ellerm's overwhelming reaction to this judicial outrage was probably relief. After his release, he returns to Great Shelford. In the 1851 census, he is still living at 12, the High Street, listing his occupation as Pauper, and rather defiantly adding, 'former thatcher'.

For his part, Samuel Hercules Taunton slips out of Cambridge and returns to London with a good deal less fanfare than that night in early January, when he had been so keen to trumpet his success. He remained a Bow Street Runner until the service was disbanded in 1839, superceded by the new Metropolitan Police Force. In retirement, Taunton tried his hand as a writer; a desperate detective indeed.[50]

As for Great Shelford, nothing more is seen of its arsonist's work for several months. John Stallon has entered a new, more restrained period of his life.

BOOK TWO

THE FIRE AT
MR WILKINSON'S

Chapter Eleven

THE COLD ICE OF SUMMER

> *Some say the world will end in fire,*
> *Some say in ice...*
>
> Robert Frost, *Fire & Ice*.

One thing I've learned in researching the lives of working people in the early 1830s is they left very little behind. They are undocumented, to use the modern term. Consequently, we know hardly anything about the lives and thoughts and feelings of men like John Stallon. Yet even with that distance taken into account, there is something cool about John. Even cold. How else could he stay silent in the months following the fire at Mr Headly's? For all of January, and all of February, Joseph Ellerm languished in prison. This was a man whose prospects were even less promising than John's own. Yet because of John's way with fire – that child's breath upon a glowing rag – poor Joe was taken from his family, thrown into Cambridge Castle, harried by his interrogator, and forced to contemplate a trial for his life. With so many in the countryside clamouring for arsonists to be dealt with severely, this – as the *Morning Herald* had noted – could so easily have led Joseph Ellerm to his grave. Thank God for Baron Gurney's pernickety insistence on evidence.

Of course, the price of confession – the consequences for Stallon's own family if he had admitted his guilt – would have been immense. Elizabeth was now heavily pregnant, and their older son not quite eight years of age. What would a sensible father and husband do in that situation? Could John afford to feel responsible for Joe Ellerm's plight?

Obviously not. John Stallon remained a closed book.

He did at least stop lighting fires, though even that was not entirely to his credit. As time went on with no further attacks, the suspicion that the man in custody was indeed guilty must have grown and grown in the minds of his fellow villagers. Once released, Joseph Ellerm's welcome back to the village was, we can imagine, muted.

In fact, once Ellerm was free, Stallon kept up his good behaviour for the whole of that year.

Between these two key dates – the morning of the fire at Rectory Farm on December 13 1831, and the next fire on January 26, 1833, John Stallon lit not a single fire, or at least none that is reported. At this stage he seems in total control of his actions.

In defence of his terrible work rate as an arsonist that year, Stallon might justifiably claim he had other things on his mind.

The first reason was the best. In April, Elizabeth's pregnancy came to a positive conclusion. A third child was born, a healthy boy. As tradition dictated, this second son was named after a close male relative, and John chose his elder brother, William. As a middle name, John and Elizabeth chose Patman – Elizabeth's family suffix – to keep that name alive, too. It's clear there was a lot riding on this new arrival. With a new baby, and with Spring in full flush, it must have felt like a new beginning for one of Great Shelford's oddest couples.

A second, truly devastating event in that year was to bring that fresh start crashing. At harvest time John's big brother Bill – that same William in whose name their baby had just been baptised – was violently killed.

The harrowing facts of Bill's slaughter, reported in *The Weekly Dispatch* at the time of the killer's eventual trial, are these: 'William Stallion' like his brother John and all agricultural labourers looked forward to harvest as a time of plentiful work and good wages. In Bill's case, he was working in Trumpington, the village lying to the north of Great Shelford, between the village and the city of Cambridge, where William lived. Heading back from the fields one evening William and his workmates stopped off at a Trumpington ale house, *The William the Fourth*. It was probably a fairly new establishment, given the name, since the King had been on the throne for less than three years. A few hours later, suitably refreshed, the group spilled onto the road. As they dragged their weary limbs homeward, one of the harvesters – a teenager called John Nightingale – began provoking Bill, suggesting 'Stallion' had stolen some chickens.

To take a rabbit or a pheasant in the fields, (though the law was bearing down even on these traditional perks), was generally accepted. To use the phrase, it was 'fair game' – a nominal crime against a landowner. Chickens however would be loosed on the commons; take one of these, and you steal from your neighbours.

Bill took exception to Nightingale's slander. He carefully laid his reaping hook down on the road and took a swing at young Nightingale. He landed what sounds like the perfect sucker punch. Reeling backwards, possibly panicked by the aggression of the older man, Nightingale drew his own reaping hook from his belt. Unsheathing the cutting edge, he challenged Bill to a fight; 'Hook in hand, life for life'.

Perhaps the older man was just too slow on his feet; perhaps he'd drunk more than he realised, or perhaps that first punch sapped his energy. The fight was a short one. John Nightingale sliced Bill Stallon's arm from wrist to elbow. Bill immediately began to lose blood at a horrifying rate but claimed not to be bothered by it. A friend was less sanguine and took Bill to his home and called for a surgeon to stitch up the wound. The doctor did his work, and at first Bill seemed to be doing well. But infection set in. The wound would take a while to trip its victim into fever. From there, it pushed him further and further into the agonies of gangrene and on to the mercy of delirium. Seven days later Bill Stallon was dead.[51]

There is a mystery here. *The Dispatch's* account is clear that the fight took place on the 8th of August, and that seven days passed before 'William Stallion' was pronounced dead. This would mean he died on the 15th August at the latest.

Burial records at St Mary the Virgin in Great Shelford show that William Stallen [sic], of Cambridge, was interred there on December 12th.

The obvious conclusion is that despite all we have learned about the free-wheeling spelling of names, William Stallon (or Stallion) and William Stallen are two different people. But the two men are of a similar age and the coincidence of the deaths seems remarkable. And why would a man from Cambridge be buried in Great Shelford, unless his family lived there?

Count the months: August, September, October, November, December…

Is it possible that a body would be held for so long before burial? Doubtful. Having said that, much is made in *The Dispatch's* account of the tireless efforts of '*the most eminent surgeons of our town and county hospital*' to save William Stallion's life. Did they hold on to the corpse afterwards? If so, for what reason?

Perhaps it was to dissect it. The Anatomy Act of 1832 gave medics wide-ranging powers over bodies. It was introduced in a bid to increase the availability of corpses for the medical profession, and to undermine the trade of grave robbers. If a cadaver remained unclaimed in a workhouse or hospital for seven days, surgeons were entitled to claim it for dissection. In fact, even prior to the Act taking effect, bodies were often used for this purpose. The Company of Surgeons shared their right to take corpses for dissection with only two other institutions in England; the Royal College of Physicians, and Caius College, Cambridge. The latter has a long association with the County Hospital – which we now know as Addenbrooke's – whose governors had declared, as far back as January 1767,

That in any doubtful case the Physicians and Surgeons shall have power to open the body of any person dying in the Infirmary without asking any Person leave.[52]

Or could the surgeons have simply been awaiting payment for stitching William up and trying to save his life? If fees were added to anticipated funeral costs, could the family have struggled to afford to reclaim his body?

At the beginning of the nineteenth century, it was certainly not unusual for a body to wait a good week or so while a family scrabbled around for funds to underwrite a funeral. The most basic funeral – at the time – Burial, dues, Church, Sexton, Bell – cost around 10s, plus refreshments for the mourners. For Labourers that was a week's wages, or more. If a stone was included, the cost was even higher.

A burial could be done cheaper than this; in some towns and villages around the UK at the time there was a parish coffin, re-used for each pauper burial. If the body was interred in a collective grave, it might only cost a shilling. And in fact, by delaying, William's funeral became increasingly expensive; in the 1830s a grave was cheaper to dig in the warmer months when the earth was soft than it was in winter when falling temperatures left the ground frosted and hard. [53]

Then again, William and his family were not paupers. They were labourers. They were no doubt keen to give Bill a decent send off, whether his cadaver had been dismembered by the surgeons or not, but in some ways, the fact that the family were not paupers made this ambition more difficult to achieve. The parish did not have the same duty to support labourers as it did the destitute.

It's also true that in the grim calendar of putrescence, there is a lot of difference between a week and five months. Is it possible that William's remains were interred at the Hospital after his death in August, and exhumed for re-burial in December, when the family had finally gathered sufficient funds?

Whatever the answer to this mystery, the story of the fight with reaping hooks reveals a lot about the violence of the times in which John Stallon and his brother lived. And, when the case of Stallion versus Nightingale finally came to court in March 1833, it tells us a great deal about the relative values of this unyielding world.

If found guilty of setting fire to Mr Headly's barns, Joseph Ellerm would have paid with his poor, 'grossly illiterate' life. For causing the death of John Stallon's brother Bill, John Nightingale was sentenced to just one year in prison (though admittedly with hard labour). The loss of a human life was significant, as the Judge who sentenced Nightingale made clear. It was nowhere near as important as the loss of property.

The icy restraint John had maintained since December 1832 would not last long once William's body was returned to Shelford. As autumn turned to winter, and William was laid to rest not far from his little niece Ann, something inside John Stallon gave.

Chapter Twelve

A SHORT MARCH TO FROG HALL

...and men loved darkness rather than light, for their deeds were evil.
The Gospel of John, Ch 3 v 19.

Exactly one hundred and eighty-nine years to the day, I set off in search of John Stallon's next target for oblivion – a place called Frog Hall, home to a farmer named William Wilkinson.

In the year 1833, January 27th fell on a Sunday. It was the habit of John and his family to go to church in the morning. Perhaps, in the afternoon, they took a walk to the river or visited Elizabeth's parents who lived in the village. At least they were assured of a meal there. By the time the little band walked home, the light would be fading. Some leftovers if they were lucky; then, with the baby in bed, and John Jr and Elizabeth settled at the fire, John slipped out of *Woodlands* cottage to pick his way through the ruined and pitch-black orchard, carefully avoiding Elizabeth's ducks. Ahead of him was a twenty-minute tramp, cross-field, to the rear of Mr Wilkinson's farmhouse in the neighbouring parish of Little Shelford. There John set about rekindling his incendiary ways.

My own journey to Mr Wilkinson's farm differs in a number of respects. The 27th of January is a Wednesday this year. Also, I lock up my bike very near the supposed site of John and Elizabeth's cottage in the morning, in good time to complete my task in daylight.

How John made his way through the inky darkness we don't know, but he had probably spent time labouring for Mr Wilkinson, and so had a good idea of the route he must follow. He would also, we must suspect, have scoped out the farm and its outbuildings on one of those earlier occasions. Useful, given what he had to accomplish.

Once through the orchard behind his tenement, John would cross Peter Grain's fields (now the village recreation ground) to reach the near side of the River Granta. If there was a footbridge in place, or some other means of reaching the other side, this stealthy figure would have crossed the water and clambered down the shallow embankment. After that, he was into the low-lying pasture and scrubby woodland that would fetch him up at Wilkinson's barns. If there was no crossing, and nothing to ferry him the few yards across the river, John would have cut right along the riverbank, following the Granta's swollen brown waters. A few minutes later he would arrive at King's Mill a quarter of a mile downstream.

This being Sunday, the great mill wheel had ceased grinding its flour for the week. Unnoticed, John could cross by the weir. In 1918 (according to Fanny Wale's sketchbook) there is a pretty little footbridge at this point, but for John it was probably a case of hanging his boots around his neck, and paddling. Once across the river, he would pass the mill-workers' low-roofed cottages on his left and could then cut across-field again. Whatever his precise means of traversing the river, the route took John Stallon through tussocky grass much given to flooding at this time of year, and then into a muddy patch still labelled on the OS map as Pudding Acre.

Two years later, the Enclosure of Great Shelford's fields would declare John's approach – even without its intended result – as trespass. And so it remains today. Consequently, I have to stick to the pavement that snakes left at the junction of Woollards Lane and Church Street, passes the Church and the *George and Dragon*, crosses not one but two branches of the river below the mill, and eventually strikes sharply left again. From Little Shelford Manor, the path hugs the long, lonely road towards Whittlesford. This last stretch – something of a nightmare for modern pedestrians – will bring me after a mile to that side of Wilkinson's farmhouse that faces the road. Or rather, it will bring me to the place where Wilkinson's farm should be. According to Fanny Wale, it lies directly opposite a very grand house called Sanfoins. Today, Sanfoins is exactly where Fanny left it; opposite, there is no farmhouse at all.

Having driven or cycled by here many times, I have two hypotheses to explain this missing farmhouse. It's possible that Fanny is once again being a little loose with her facts. It could be that she is referring to the buildings a little further along Whittlesford Road, now known as Rectory Farm, Little Shelford.

This farmhouse is quite a pretty one: you can see why later owners might change its name from Frog Hall.

The other possibility, one I am keen to check out, is that what remains of Frog Hall lies along a track I've noticed running perpendicular to the road, bisecting the fields between Little Shelford Farm (the farm closest to the village), and Rectory Farm further on. The track is marked on the map and clearly visible in the real world as it strikes off in the direction of Pudding Acre. It ends abruptly 100 yards on. Could it be that Mr Wilkinson's Frog Hall has been razed to the ground? Might there be some clues at the end of the track, even after 189 years?

The final difference between John Stallon's walk and mine (apart from its degree of muddiness, the time of day, and its ultimate goal – I am very deliberately not carrying matches) is that I am accompanied by my Wire-haired Dachsund, Stig. He is unaware of the walk's greater significance but is just as keen as I am to explore the track to our left.

It has taken Stig and his owner thirty minutes to walk from the centre of Great Shelford to the mouth of the track that leads – perhaps – to Frog Hall. I realise I have a decision to make.

Rectory Farm is a further quarter of a mile along a road that manages to be both busy with speeding traffic and desolate for the walker. In my pocket I have a letter of introduction for the people of Rectory Farm, requesting their help with my research. Maybe they can tell me if the farm was ever renamed? That would be the normal, formal, respectful approach for a researcher.

I could blame it on Stig's impatience or say that John Stallon's subterfuge is baiting me to follow his example, but the responsibility is clearly my own; I drop my shoulder and head away from the road along the hedgerow in the gloom of this grey, overcast morning, in search of the ruins of Mr Wilkinson's farm.

★

Whether John Stallon set off that evening with the express intention of ending his twelve-month fire-fast, we cannot know. Generally, he lit fires in places that were convenient to him. Why else would he hit Mr Headly's property so many times? Four times, in total. When, later, he was questioned by those looking for a malicious motive John repeatedly said he harboured no grudge towards his Master at all. Quite the opposite. It seems that he torched property belonging to Headly mainly because all he had to do was turn up for work at first light, and make sure he was the first to get there. That way he could set his fire before his fellow workers showed up and was well positioned to sound the alarm when they did.

How John felt about William Wilkinson as an employer, we don't know for sure, but a clue appears in a report on the ensuing fire that appeared in the *Bury & Norwich Gazette* on Weds 30th January 1833:

Mr W. had lowered his labourer's wages the previous morning…

it says, adding some information that highlights the tough life for paupers in the Shelfords:

> *...there are at this time in that parish between 30 and 40 men employed upon the roads, who cannot earn more than four shillings a week.*

Mr Wilkinson is the hiring farmer – and this is quite plainly a hirer's market. The farmer decides unilaterally to lower the rate for the job; if you don't want to work for the reduced wage, there are plenty more who will.

Given the difficulty of crossing the river in the dark, and then traversing the morass of Pudding Acre, it seems unlikely that John's walk to Frog Hall began as a pleasure trip. Payback then, pure and premeditated. Once in the farmyard, full of shadows, John's muscle memory kicks in. The same is true of the barn. The huge shed looming before him obligingly remembers how to blaze.

The decision was also likely, it seems to me, to be a pragmatic one, and calculated. Stallon was later adamant that he did what he did a dozen times, chiefly for the money. The reward for raising the alarm and helping to man the engine was six shillings and sixpence.[54] In 1833 that was just over half a week's wages. Baby William was ten months old; his brother John Jr was now a growing boy of going-on nine years. On a Sunday evening, with the whole week to get through in a month when the weather was pinched and the amount of farmwork scarce, income was the same – and now Farmer Wilkinson had dropped the wages on offer. There was perhaps only one thought in John's head. He and Elizabeth had mouths to feed. As he had already discovered, nothing raised money like dousing a fire.

What did John say to Elizabeth by way of explanation as he left home that dark Sunday evening? What did *she* say when he eventually came back? That would be later the following day, and John would be reeking of smoke, with enormous muddy moonboots on his feet. Of course, Elizabeth would have heard the alarm, seen the smoke again, been alert to all the other signs of panic in the village. As she dutifully scraped off John's footwear, did she keep tight-lipped for fear the children would hear the row brewing between them? Or did she embrace her beloved John when he slunk back in, pleased at least that he had joined the chase with the engine? Or earlier, when he went out, did she sink to the floor as the door clunked shut, fist in her mouth for terror, knowing the danger to which her desperate but determined husband was about to expose their family?

Elizabeth needn't have worried. Not yet. John had chosen his target well, and his timing was perfect.

Once again, news of the latest act of incendiarism plaguing the Shelfords flew around the country. Even in the Welsh borders it made the newspapers. The *Hereford Journal* of 6 February 1833 (relaying an account from the *Cambridge Chronicle*) reported that Wilkinson's farm was three-quarters of a mile from the church in Great Shelford, and that the '*neighbourhood was filled with alarm*' as the fire at Frog Hall '*raged with great fury*'. The road that I had walked – 189 years too late to witness anything more dramatic than speeding traffic – was in 1833 the only feasible route down which to drag, push and cajole the fire engine, housed at St Mary the Virgin.

Again, another tender attended from an insurance company, (in this case the Norwich Union), and again the fire was contained. Nonetheless the losses to the farmer were significant. '...*a large barn containing wheat and barley, a quantity of threshed wheat, barley and oats, a large haystack and several stacks of straw...*' – all were destroyed. Mercifully, as in the fire at Mr Headly's, no one was harmed. Mercifully too, the farmer had the comfort of his insurance pay-out to look forward to, this time to the tune of £800. And again 'the powers that be' would be shaken by this outrage – and determine to leap into action.

★

When he returns to the cottage, John is too exhausted to leap anywhere. His lungs are again full of smoke, and there is no mistaking the anxiety on Elizabeth's face. But John's pocket jangles with the sound of many church bells, in the form of six shillings and sixpence.

★

My unofficial saunter down the short track leading me away from the road to Whittlesford in search of Frog Hall, reveals little. The track itself is a very sound one – a considerable investment by someone. That suggests it once had more to do than simply admit a tractor into the fields. It ends though in a scrub of trees and brush. There are no foundations that I can see, poking through that brush; no partial walls, no concrete pan or house bricks that might suggest there was ever a farmhouse, or a farmyard at the end of the track, let alone one from the nineteenth century. Despite the effort and expense in building it, the track is, today at any rate, the proverbial road to nowhere. Stig and I double back and press on to Rectory Farm. We knock on the door, but no one answers; the farmer or farmers are working. I push my letter of introduction-cum-research through the flap, and head home.

★

Some days later, I realise I owe Fanny Wale an apology. True, her directions to Frog Hall are a bit loose, but her description of the farmhouse in other sections of her book – including the fact that a footpath (an official one) runs hard by the farm taking the walker directly to Sawston, leave me in no doubt; Rectory Farm *is* Frog Hall, renamed. A map from 1816 (the time of Little Shelford's Enclosure) predates Fanny's book by a hundred years. Curiously it labels the farm with the newer, more respectable name; I suppose the locals who told Fanny the story of John Stallon and his reign of terror called the farm 'Frog Hall' because that's what they always called it – gentrification or no.

Regardless of the name of its target, the Firestarter's reign of terror had now been rebooted. The response to it was also familiar.

Chapter Thirteen

COMETH THE HOUR, COMETH THE MAGISTRATE.

> *There is a tide in the affairs of men,*
> *Which, taken at the flood, leads on to*
> *   fortune;*
> *Omitted, all the voyage of their life*
> *Is bound in shallows and in miseries.*
>
> *Julius Caesar* by William Shakespeare

There is something 'bound in shallows' about the Reverend Edward Serocold Pearce. To use another image, he has always laboured in the shadow of others – principally, his father. William Pearce was a famous and long serving Master of Jesus College Cambridge. For the last twenty-three years of his life, he was simultaneously the Dean of Ely Cathedral – and was also a Fellow of the Royal Society. Today, his portrait hangs in the National Portrait Gallery. Not surprisingly, his son Edward struggles to measure up.

Edward has had his triumphs. In 1832 he published a collection of Bible stories, retold for the young, honing each tale by reading them to his children – or maybe at them. And he has served for a number of years as a magistrate, a field where he feels he might do some good. In fact, he was one of the vicar-magistrates recruited by the Earl of Hardwicke to carry out his *Inquiry into the Actual State and Condition of the Poor in every Parish in the County*, in 1830. More recently, Edward has found a new cause, striving to make the name Serocold (his mother's maiden name) officially part of his own name. In a few years' time in 1842, he will finally obtain a Royal Licence to do so. It is hard not see that particular quest – and Edward's determined pursuit of it – as a rather defensive nailing of his colours to the maternal mast.[55]

Pearce *père* is alas, now dead, and Edward's mother is snoring just along the corridor. Edward shares this rather grand house in Benet Place, Cambridge with his wife and children as well as his mother. Tonight, as his mother shakes the rafters and the rest of the family try to sleep, Edward paces the floor of his study with increasingly frantic steps. He is trying to keep at bay what we might recognise from our own terrifying moments of anguish as the unmistakeable beginnings of a panic attack.

A few days previously, on hearing about the fire at Mr Wilkinson's farm in Little Shelford – and knowing the Earl of Hardwicke was currently indisposed – Edward Pearce had decided he must become a man of action. As the Earl previously confided in him, the secret of good governance is to both consider and to act. Edward stored that piece of advice like a squirrel with a nut and, on the day of the fire at Little Shelford, he bit down hard. He immediately applied to the office of the Home Secretary for advice and consideration in the matter. Once he had received that advice, he acted without delay, calling up to Shelford a Principal Officer recommended by Mr Phillips, Viscount Melbourne's Secretary. And so another Bow Street Runner had arrived in Cambridgeshire on the trail of the Shelford arsonist.

A week later, Pearce wrote to Lord Melbourne to appraise him of events, and to solicit further assistance. Serocold's letters – again tracked down in the National Archive at Kew – tend to the long and fussy and, schooled by his life among giants, just a tiny bit obsequious. To his credit, his handwriting is far more legible than the Earl of Hardwicke's:

My Lord

After I had the honour of waiting on Your Lordship on Sunday the 27th of January [respecting?] the fire at Little Shelford in this County, I obtained in consequence of an order from Mr Phillips, the assistance of Leadbitter, the Police Officer.

Leadbitter has no doubt that we have the incendiary now in custody, but we meet with the utmost difficulty in getting any facts to prove the charge.

Under these circumstances, though we have found rewards of £500 useless in other cases, there seems ground to hope that some of the labourers who are [now?] unwilling to speak out, may be induced to come forward by a tolerable reward.

The farmers hope to make up £100 pounds tonight; at all events I will personally guarantee the reward shall not be under £50; and the object of my present application is to request most respectfully that your Lordship will be pleased to authorise me to offer an additional reward from His Majesty's Government if it should appear to be such a proper case for interposition.

I should not have written until I had ascertained the exact amount subscribed had it not been that our Petty Sessions for the division are held here on Saturday, and the hope of tonight's post could permit the bills being issued on Friday.

I have the honour to be, my Lord, your Lordship's most obedient, humble servant.

E. Serocold Pearce,
Benet Place, Cambridge
February 6, 1833 [56]

Ah, the age-old complaint of the law: there is '*no doubt that we have the incendiary now in custody, but we meet with the utmost difficulty in getting any facts to prove the charge*'.

In fact, George Leadbitter had moved as swiftly as his

predecessor and Bow Street colleague Samuel Taunton to arrest his suspect – or rather suspects. In the aftermath of the fire at Mr Wilkinson's, Leadbitter had initially detained not one, but three Little Shelford labourers on a charge of arson. After further questioning, the youngest of the three, a twenty-year old named John Astell was released. The remaining two suspects were now safely held in Mr Orridge's prison at Cambridge Castle.

Although only recently making the rank of Principal Officer, George Leadbitter had, like SHT, come up through the ranks, having previously served in the foot patrol. Before that, he had been a gardener. His is a large, commanding figure – often deployed in facing down crowds at race meetings or breaking up illegal fist fights. It is not, though, Serocold's sudden acquaintance with this physical giant that has shaken him to his boots this evening, but the whirlwind of events that have beset both men in the previous seventy-two hours. That, and the half pile of handbills, fresh from the printers – handbills that now lie face down on Serocold's desk. If Serocold had his wish, it would not only be barns that disappeared in a ball of flame.

As the *Huntingdon, Bedford and Peterborough Gazette* reports on Saturday 9 February 1833, with the usual cavalier spelling of names, all had not gone to plan for the Rev Pearce and officer Leadbitter:

We regret to state, that while the Rev. Serecold Pearce, (a magistrate of the county) assisted by Leadbeater, of London, were examining some suspects in the above village [Shelford] some daring ruffians had the audacity to fire a stack, on the premises of Mr Headley, and a stable, gig-house and store-rooms, in the occupation of Mr Carter, in the immediate neighbourhood of the scene...

Two additional fires ignited even as Pearce and Leadbitter

were questioning the newly-detained Shelford Three; Rev Pearce's bold assurance to Lord Melbourne – that the arsonists are already in custody – suddenly looks very suspect.

Undeterred, Serocold had again chosen to act. Quick as a flash, he intercepted the handbill before it left the printers and insisted on a clutch of amendments. The subject of the handbill is thus no longer 'Fire at Shelford', but 'Fires..'. Now the wording in clear black and white, reads as follows:

Fires at Shelford

Mr Wilkinson's Farm, Jan 26th
Mr Headly's Stacks AND Mr Carter's Stable
LAST NIGHT

£300
Is offered for such Information as shall lead to the
Conviction of the **INCENDIARIES**

AND

His Majesty's
PARDON
Will be granted to any
ACCOMPLICE

who not having himself set fire to any of the above

property shall be the means of the principal

Offender or Offenders being brought to justice.

Cambridge, Friday, February 8, 1833.

[Wilson, Printer, Bridge-Street, Cambridge.] [57]

Edward had dropped off a little over half the redrawn handbills to fellow magistrates on the way home. Only that night, as he sat down to view the printer's work with satisfaction, did it dawn on him he had compounded one error with another. The pardon offered by the King applied only to the first fire – his poster offers it for information on any of the three.

Best to come clean. Picking up a pen and ink again, he writes out a second letter to the mighty Viscount Melbourne. Serocold concentrates hard to keep his hand steady, and his mode of expression transparent:

My Lord,

I had the honour of receiving your Lordship's authority this morning, in a letter from Mr Phillips, to add £50 to the reward offered for the detection of the fire at Shelford, & to make known His Majesty's Pardon in case any [?] should come forward.

I regret to state that two more fires took place last night: one at Great Shelford, the other at Little Shelford: a straw stack on the Tithe Farm of Mr Headly, and a range of stabling occupied by a University man, was destroyed.

I was there with Leadbitter some time after the first fire burnt out, and until both were extinguished, and am sorry to say all our enquiries are at present fruitless, though it is quite clear that many persons are in the [?] of the first of all the fires on the 26th January.

Mr Headly's is the farm which was almost totally destroyed by fire a year and half ago.

Under these circumstances I humbly hope that your Lordship will not think that I have done wrong in joining all the fires together in the enclosed hand bill, though the pardon was authorised only in the former case...

To be fair, Serocold wasn't alone in linking the fires. The newspapers had already come to the same conclusion. But Serocold knows he has made an error. In his anxiety to act, he has failed to accurately relay the terms of a Royal Pardon. If someone should implicate the destroyer of Mr Carter's stable, or Mr Headly's haulm stack, and attempt to claim the reward, the Crown would have every right to refuse. Serocold could find himself liable. Worse, an informant clutching a copy of the handbill might curse the King for publishing false promises – and Serocold would again be culpable.

Somewhere in the back of Edward's head, a voice is suggesting he has, once again – and oh, SO characteristically – overreached himself.

We can be pretty sure the voice is that of his father.

Swallowing hard, Edward reaches for more ink and adds to his second letter a wealth of detail about the sums of money, and their respective sources, which now combine in the reward offered. He is desperate to show he is not being casual with the King's money, or anyone's money – to be casual about anything is certainly not in Serocold's nature. And then he returns to the matter gnawing at his insides:

> ... *I am anxious to know that, in this extraordinary case, your Lordship excuses the steps I have taken respecting the pardon...*

Adding, as if in mitigation...

> *...the affairs of these parishes...are in great confusion.*
> *I have the honour to be, my Lord, your Lordship's most obedient, humble...*[58]

...and so on.

The second letter completed, and despatched, the Reverend Pearce may have considered this unfortunate disaster – albeit one entirely of his own making – averted. Once again, he has acted swiftly, and with the utmost propriety. He has confessed his error. He can only hope that his reputation as a reliable and astute Magistrate, and as an honourable servant of the Crown, will survive this whole sorry episode.

What Reverend Pearce does not mention in his letter – and does not realise will soon be revealed in the newspapers – is that it is not only the parish of Little Shelford that is in confusion – or indeed the handbill, still tacky to the touch. It is the whole of the investigation that he and Leadbitter have launched that is teetering on the brink of farce.

In the first place, the fire at Mr Carter's has been found to be not the work of a desperate incendiary but a complete accident. A fourteen-year-old boy called George Clark, employed as a stable boy, has come forward to confess he left a candle burning untended in the stable.

In the second place, the men that Pearce and Leadbitter had taken into custody for the original fire, had broken out of their cell in Cambridge Castle and made a bid for freedom.

Whatever the response from Lord Melbourne to Serocold's flurry of correspondence, the whole saga is fast becoming an unmitigated shambles.

Chapter Fourteen

IF ONLY THE STONES COULD SPEAK...

Man of peace or man of war
The peacock spreads his fan.
Leonard Cohen, *The Story of Isaac*.

The agricultural labourers Robert Elborne and Joseph Shearing were nothing if not resourceful. Imprisoned in the County Gaol at Cambridge Castle, they would have been relieved that their prolonged questioning by Magistrate Pearce and the police officer Leadbitter on Wednesday 6 February had resulted in the release of their young workmate, John Ansell. On the other hand, their continued detainment suggests that no matter how much they protest their own innocence, they are not going to be believed. They have been told they will face further questioning the following Saturday.

The thought of spending three more nights in a cell shared with some of the county's least successful criminals, is not a good one. At the end of those three nights, they will face another barrage of futile questions from the Magistrate, while Leadbitter paces behind them, cracking his knuckles. And all the time they are not in the fields. If men like them do not toil, they do not earn. It is more than decent men can bear.

And so they do the obvious, if not the decent, thing. Finding a piece of wood, they fashion a skeleton key, and with the cell door swinging wide behind them, they simply walk out of prison.

Due to the prompt action of Mr Orridge, the prison governor, they are detained again almost immediately – before they can breach the outer wall, in fact. They are promptly flung back inside.

Now their position is if anything, even more desperate. They have annoyed the prison governor and potentially embarrassed both the police officer from London and the Magistrate who has the power to send them to the assizes. But at least they have done what they could to help themselves. Honour, if honour is worth anything these days, has been satisfied.

Meanwhile, back in Shelford, whoever is the real incendiary is causing a steady stream of chaos. To set fire to Mr Wilkinson's farm – the first attack in Little Shelford rather than Great – was quite a stroke. But to light three fires inside a fortnight is beginning to look like attention seeking. And perhaps that is the point.

Having cast doubt on John Stallon's bravery or empathetic capacity in allowing Joe Ellerm to languish in his place, it is only right that we consider the possibility that Stallon was now consciously trying to undermine the case against Shearing and Elborne. It was after all, entirely possible that John Stallon considered these two men workmates. Friends, even. Elborne was just two years his senior; like John, a husband and a father. In fact, Robert had an elder brother William Elborne, and also a cousin of the same name, born in the same year. One of these William Elbornes served as a witness at John and Elizabeth's wedding in 1820. Joe Shearing was a little younger, but he too had a family. Joe's wife, another Elizabeth, had given birth to a daughter Phoebe, just 17 months earlier. Although from different villages, the three men almost certainly knew each other and had probably worked together at Wilkinson's farm. It is hard to believe that John, once he realised that his flare-up at Frog Hall had triggered the arrest of these innocent workmates, would be completely unmoved by their plight. It is not much harder to believe he might try to compensate – in the only way he knew how, with fire.

I picture him in the church of St Mary the Virgin back in

Great Shelford – perhaps after the engine has been returned to its station in the church porch. Outside, the further fires inflicted on poor Mr Headly and Mr Carter, were now extinguished. I see him staring hard at the whitewashed walls, as if seeking assurance that his shot at redemption would be noticed. Perhaps he would even be praying that his attempts at distraction will prove effective; that little Phoebe will get her father back.

For some reason, whenever he sat in church, those whitewashed walls seemed to John to almost pulsate with meaning – far more meaning than Rev Finch's sermons ever did. And yet they remain blank, saying nothing.

Years after Stallon's death, a new broom of a vicar arrived in Great Shelford and determined to restore its crumbling church. Only then would the whitewash covering the walls be stripped back. In that moment, in 1868, the entire panoply of judgement was revealed, painted onto the archway over the chancel. In one of the best-preserved Doom paintings in England, dating from the 15th century, the fates of the saved and the unsaved are depicted as they face Final Judgement; the righteous going away to heaven, and the impenitent cast into eternal flame. If he had seen it, would John Stallon have realised where his own fire-raising might lead? Would he have changed his ways? Or, is it possible he would go one better, noticing how this vision of heaven reflected so many earthly realities? Some, like the Rev Edward Serocold Pearce strode the earth dispensing judgement, while others like Shearing, Elborne, Ellerm – and himself if he wasn't careful – had 'justice' thrust upon them. The appeal of religion was clear; until there was real justice on earth, the only hope was you might get luckier in heaven. Why not, instead, light fires with a real purpose – beyond the six shillings and sixpence you earned for putting them out? Better still, light no fires at all, but organise with those with whom you had common interest, and work for a change in the world, loosening the grip of the Masters on every worker's life. Alas, all Stallon could see was the church's whitewash.

The ecclesiastical and the spiritual should not, of course, be confused. Back in 1833, perhaps Stallon's heart did go out to God, and perhaps those prayers were answered.

After that final session of questioning the following Saturday, the Rev Pearce seems to have concluded there was not enough evidence to commit Shearing and Elborne to the Assizes. He had doubtless heard about the Grand Jury's scathing verdict of 'No True Bill' in response to SHT's efforts to try Joseph Ellerm. The lighting of more fires while the suspects were in prison, the error over the King's Pardon, the suspects near-escape from prison, and to cap it all, the business of the stableboy and the candle – all these had taken their toll. Enough of the embarrassments. There was little to do but pay Officer George Leadbitter his expenses and release the two skeleton-key-whittling labourers back into the wild.

The Shelford Arsonist had, undoubtedly, won another round.

Besides, there were other cases needing the Reverend's attention. On Saturday February 16th, the *Huntingdon, Bedford & Peterborough Gazette* reports that in Cambridge, the Reverend Edward Serocold Pearce has committed to the Town Prison a young man name John Nightingale – to await trial, charged with slaying one William Stallion. In one case at least, the Reverend might deliver something like justice.

Chapter Fifteen

LIKE SEARCHING FOR A NEEDLE IN A HAYSTACK

...one philosopher pointed out that though the position of the poor man might seem wanting in dignity or independence, it should be remembered by way of consolation that he could play the tyrant over his wife and children as much as he liked.

JL Hammond and Barbara Hammond, *The Village Labourer, 1760-1832*

'Hello, anybody home?'
No response. The well-dressed woman glances around. Sarah Wright, Elizabeth's neighbour, does not seem to be at home either. Sarah Cambridge pushes open the door to Elizabeth Stallon's downstairs room and waits while her eyes adjust to the dark. Stygian gloom, a book would call it.

Sarah is on her own now. Her husband Thomas, the father of her children, is one of Old Cambridge's sons, the youngest of four brothers. The oldest son, William Cambridge Jr, also married a Sarah, who being a widow is now also on her own. Both women are called Sarah Cambridge, so that sometimes causes confusion. The older woman is a Schoolmistress, up on High Green. This Sarah Cambridge – the one who is poised on Elizabeth's threshold – has been known to help out at the school as a favour to her sister-in-law, the other Sarah Cambridge, but there is not really work for them both. Besides, Sarah, our Sarah, has four children of her own plus her elderly parents-in-law to wrangle. She picked up that role after Thomas, her husband, was sentenced to seven years transportation for theft. His sentence was eventually commuted to a year's hard labour but he is currently dodging that with a spell in the navy. Even when he was at home he was never much to rely on.

In the meantime, Sarah looks after Old William and Hannah, cares for her own children, and tries to stay cheerful. Elizabeth Stallon can usually be counted on for a little peace and quiet, a little companionship.

Not today. It's clear the house is empty.

Now her eyes have adjusted, Sarah can see to put her gifts away.

For weeks she has tried to persuade Elizabeth to give up lighting the little range with a tinderbox. 'Lucifers' have been available for a while. They stink of sulphur and can fizz a bit, but you can pick them up for a few coppers. The time and effort a box of matches would save poor Elizabeth would be well worth the investment, but for some reason her friend cannot fathom, Elizabeth is not keen. She is probably afraid John Junior will get hold of them and cause mischief. Well, now Elizabeth has a handful of Lucifers and her knees will surely be grateful.

Sarah slips the matches into the little wooden box where she knows Elizabeth keeps her 'treasures' – a few favourite buttons and a prayerbook she can't read – out of the way of little hands. The rest of the things Sarah brought with her – a few old clothes Elizabeth might be able to make use of – can be left on the table. Elizabeth is demon with a needle, her tiny fingers good at plotting insanely neat stitches on a hem or a mend. Good job with a man like John Stallon in your life, forever coming home with ashburns in his clothes from working the engine.

The last thing in the bag is a book. For quite a few weeks last winter Sarah spent time helping John with his reading. She wasn't really teaching him, he'd learned his alphabet at Sunday school, but reading is a habit you can lose. Practise, practise, practise. He was painfully slow at first, but not too proud to learn, like most men. And he'd started to come alive, full of confidence as one and then another intimidating page of close print faltered and cracked under pressure from his gaze. Sarah was reminded of an address she'd read from the Norfolk Assizes where the judge – a certain Justice Gurney – had described education among the labouring classes as 'a mighty engine'. The judge had warned that such learning must be clearly linked to sound instruction. People must be taught their duty to God, and to their neighbour, enabling them to become good subjects, good Christians, and good citizens. Otherwise, a county like Norfolk – or Cambridgeshire – was only storing up trouble for itself in educating workers – especially if there was no work and poor wages and the price of bread always rising. [59]

Sarah smiled at the thought. No danger of John Stallon not working; he was always first at any job according to Elizabeth, and the first to be hired too. And a more sober churchman was hard to imagine. Maybe a bit too sober. Bright mind, dull imagination was Sarah's diagnosis. No wonder Elizabeth sometimes looked a little wistful when Sarah had a new dress or brought some flowers round.

It was strange being in someone else's house. A friend's house is still their private place; without them being there it was odd. And intriguing.

Sarah's own husband, Thomas, called himself a carpenter like his father when they married. She'd had to marry him when she fell with her own Elizabeth, and two years later – the same year her son William was born – John Stallon and Elizabeth Patman surprised everyone by getting married to each other, and for the same reason. Sarah had grown up with John Stallon, they were the same age although since she was a Woollard (after whom the lane was named) they'd not exactly been at the same level. Elizabeth she'd known of, but she was a few years older even than Thomas, so they hadn't moved in the same circles. You couldn't really miss Elizabeth. Now here they were all these years later, John and Elizabeth

married with two children and Sarah effectively a widow,
living opposite each other.

And here she was now, halfway up her friend's staircase.
She paused to listen, but there was nothing, just a mouse
scrabbling lightly in the thatch. She climbed a few more steps
to the top of the stairs. Haulm sacks full of straw filled the
surprisingly airy upstairs space. The straw was quite fresh, but
there was a hint of woodsmoke about everything in this house.
It was obvious straight away which was John and Elizabeth's
mattress, nearest-to, and which was John Junior's over in the
corner. The baby slept with his parents still, though she knew
Elizabeth was trying to move on from that. Sarah imagined
the boys would be sharing a bed soon. She couldn't imagine
John Junior much caring for that. Smiling at the thought, she
turned to go back downstairs – and froze.

She had not even heard the door open, let alone seen John
Junior come in.

He hasn't seen her. Should she take the initiative?

By doing what?

Before she has time to compute, the boy moves to his
mother's rag bag hanging on a hook near the stove. Then he is
doing it, tearing a rag in half, and then in a strip again. Barely
nine years old and already so focussed on his task and so
capable, like a working man in miniature. The sheet or shirt
reduced to a satisfactory bundle of strips, the boy pushes them
down inside his trousers then turns and locks eyes with her.

For a moment, neither moves. The boy then turns and
walks out of the house, closing the door behind him. Still
frozen, Sarah hears him running off down the path and into
the lane.

For a long time, Sarah Cambriidge sits on a chair in
Elizabeth's downstairs room, wondering what to do. If
Elizabeth came in she could pretend she'd not long arrived,
and was only just dropping off the bag. She'd have to explain
about the matches, but that would be ok, Elizabeth would

understand if she said she'd popped them into her box for safe keeping. But how to understand what she'd seen? Does John Jr have a friend who is wounded? Why else would he need bandages?

Sarah decides to keep her own counsel. If the boy himself or a friend is in trouble it will come out, one way or the other. Her own boys are a bit older; she can find a way to ask them what they've heard without raising suspicion. Resolved, Sarah slips out of the house, glances about to check she isn't being watched, and trots quietly back across the road.

BOOK THREE

THE FIRE AT MR HEADLY'S (AGAIN), MR PAYNE'S, THE OTHER MR HEADLY'S, OLD CAMBRIDGE'S, MR KIRBY & MR TUNWELL'S, PETER GRAIN'S SHEEP PEN; AND THE ATTEMPTED FIRE AT WILLIAM DEAN'S.

Chapter Sixteen

TO CONSIDER, AND TO ACT

July 19, 1841, Monday – Did nothing.
John Clare, Diary entry, while living in the
General Lunatic Asylum, Northampton.

The Hadley Centre at the Met Office is home to the Central England Tables (CET), the longest running instrumental weather record in the world. Established in 1953, it draws on data collected over many years by both professional weather-watchers and amateurs, the earliest of whom reported their findings in 1659. The CET data reveals that the weather in central England in the Spring of 1833 was remarkable. It still seems remarkable today. In the more than 360 years since the records began, the hottest mean temperature for any month of May is for the searing May of 1833. A mean average temperature of 15.1° centigrade (+4°c above the average for the entire set) left the inhabitants of middle England sweltering. It was dry, too, with barely a third of the usual rainfall.

To begin with, people in Great Shelford were no doubt glad of the sunshine. They had not long shaken off one of the wettest Februarys on record, and March and April had not been much better. In fact, the weather pattern throughout that year was bizarre. A dry January, that drenching February (which weirdly, was warmer than March), a scorching May, a wettish Summer, a mild autumn.

John Stallon's resolve in the first quarter of 1833 seems likewise to have waxed and waned – in his case, between contemplation and action. It was as well that he trod carefully.

These were to be John Stallon's last few months of liberty.

The fires at Mr Headly's farm and Mr Carter's stables in January may well have helped undermine George Leadbitter's case against John's fellow labourers Joseph Shearing and Robert Elborne, prompting their release from Cambridge Castle. Leadbitter – like Taunton before him – had returned to London in defeat, and the hue and cry from those fires quickly died down. Then John struck again at Rectory Farm in Great Shelford. It was toward the end of that long, wet February, on the 25th, a Monday; John began the fire in Henry Headly's cart shed this time. Perhaps, at first, he was simply sheltering from the rain.

In March, action turned to inaction as John's resolve abandoned him – or, to give it a more positive spin, John Stallon got a grip on his incendiary urges. Either way, (to paraphrase John Clare's diary entry above), in March 1833, John Stallon did nothing.

Once again, other events may have distracted him. March was the month when the case concerning his brother William's manslaughter finally came to court. The truth about the relative values of a farmer's property versus a man's life – and by implication, John's own life, the lives of his children and all he loved – became inescapable. The lack of proportion, the cheapness of a labourer's life, the impossibility of improving the situation you were born into – these must have impressed themselves deeply upon William's still-grieving brother.

When, in April, John began to light fires again, it seems he couldn't stop.

★

I have been thinking a lot about Elizabeth. How much did she know, or want to know, about the path John was hurtling down?

There is a possibility that Elizabeth Stallon was an active

accomplice. At the very least, I am convinced she must have been aware of John's actions. She is not stupid.

Probably, I realise, I am mapping on to Elizabeth what I know of the women in my own life. Perceptive, determined, resilient women – my mother, my wife, my sisters – but also, in my mother's case at least, a woman who often deferred to her husband.

Physically, the two women are not dissimilar. We are not a tall family, but my mother was the smallest of us all, under five feet tall. As she grew older, she grew smaller; bones, softened by twist and collapse. We used to joke that Mum would never die, just become more portable. Of course we were fooling ourselves, because we loved her.

Years ago, when my father was a Sergeant in the Royal Air Force he was in charge of the store at an airbase in Norfolk. To his lifelong shame, he fiddled the books. He said he did this to ensure his mates didn't lose pay or privileges for lost uniform or kit. He was found out, 'lost his stripes', and spent a chastening few weeks in military prison. Mum – a demon with a needle – had often been in the store, altering clothes for the lads on the base, and even some officers. Like Elizabeth, she was good with a needle; nobody could get the shape into a dress uniform the way Jane could.

Did she know what Dad was doing? Did she know he was slipping a new field cap across the counter and like her, subtly altering figures to maintain appearances?

You know your Dad, she told me when I asked, he was always up to something.

It's true; Dad was a small-time, good-hearted rogue. His education effectively finished in his early teens, when during the Blitz, his school was commandeered as a fire-station. With only his wits to rely on, Brian was always full of chat and always on the lookout for the main chance – not like John Stallon at all. But this is about Elizabeth, and Mum. No one could ever pull the wool over Jane's eyes – her four children certainly never could. But out of fear, out of lack of confidence, out of love or socially approved deference – I think Mum could occasionally pull the wool over her own eyes. Like the rest of us, she was capable of deciding that sometimes, it is better not to know.

Either way, with hungry mouths to feed the extra money finding its way into Elizabeth's house must have seemed mercurial in its timing. 'The Lord provides' didn't come close.

Chapter Seventeen

THE FIRESTARTER RAMPANT

I'm the fear addicted, a danger illustrated
I'm a firestarter...
The Prodigy, *Firestarter*

The teenager John Nightingale was convicted of the manslaughter of William Stallion on March 14, 1833 (sentence: one year with hard labour). The next crime John Stallon committed was at Henry Headly's brother's place – the second time he had targeted William Headly. That was one month later, on Saturday April 13th, 1833. The arsonist struck at 6pm in the evening. The property destroyed was William Headly's haulm stack, one of those piles of pea or corn stalks being eked out as winter feed.

The next target – just five days later – was a barn belonging to Joseph Payne, a small farmer whose patch of land lay close to William Headly's much bigger property, at the northern end of the village. That was on Thursday April 18th. The fire this time was discovered in the middle of the morning. The judgement carried by the national newspapers is now very clear – Great Shelford has become 'this ill-fated village'. [60]

Nine days later, the Shelford Arsonist strikes again. The target this time is very close to John and Elizabeth's own home in the centre of the village, and this time the fire lights up the night. A barn belonging to John and Elizabeth's ex-landlord, William Cambridge, is quickly wreathed in smoke and flames.

The acceleration in frequency, the boldness of striking in broad daylight or in the darkest hours, speaks of confidence, of compulsion, or of fury.

William Cambridge's farm is just across the road from *Woodlands* cottage where John and Elizabeth live with John Junior and baby William. Newspapers report that a cottage on the farm itself, *'containing two families'* who were sleeping at the time, was lucky to escape the reaching flames. The newspaper account also notes that only *'the prompt assistance of neighbours'* had saved the fire from spreading. The nearness of his target may be terrifying, but John's *modus operandi* is holding fast. [61]

All the same, Stallon now knows he has to be even more agile to avoid detection. Fortunately for him, the timing and target of the fire make no difference to the pay he collects for helping with the engine. In the month of April alone he must have earned nineteen shillings and sixpence for his work on the engine – a week and a half's wages – and still suspicion does not fall his way.

And yet, the old struggle between passionate action and cool calculation flickered on. John almost made it to the end of the next month – that exceptionally hot, dry May – without torching anything. But it couldn't last. On the 23rd of May, a Thursday, he struck again, this time at a barn shared by two local farmers, William Kirby and Henry Tunwell. It was late in afternoon, almost evening – though now of course it was Spring; unlike the evening in January when he'd fired Mr Wilkinson's barn at Frog Hall, he did not have cover of darkness. This left him vulnerable, as did his neighbours' extreme tension in the face of the maddening campaign they believed was being waged against them. The village Constable, Samuel Holder, was on especially high alert – and John Stallon was seen acting suspiciously.

I imagine that sometime during the earlier weeks of May, when the arid heat made everyone hyper-aware of the dryness of their thatch, and the ease with which fire might rip through the village, leading figures gathered to determine some plan of action. John Stallon, being a trusted worker and solid citizen, may even have appeared on the margins of such a meeting. It may have been held in a pub – the *Black Swan* or the *George and Dragon* since they were the most central. More likely, it being so hot, the meeting was held outside, perhaps in the yard of Rectory Farm, where so many fires had been started, close enough to bring ale from the *George* if ale was required.

The Headlys would be there of course, (Henry and William, brother with brother), and Thomas Stacey too, an early victim of the arsonist and another of Shelford's 'Big Four'. But the chief mover, the voice above all other voices would undoubtedly be that of Peter Grain.

★

A plaque in the church of St Mary the Virgin celebrates the life of Peter Grain. In particular, it commends him for the *'…upright and conscientious discharge of his duty in every relation of life.'* This generosity of spirit is not always evident in his words.

Peter Grain's opinion on the labouring classes is a matter of record. In 1832, The Royal Commission into the Operation of the Poor Laws saw commissioners fanning out across the country in pursuit of facts on the ground. The interviews they conducted would form the basis of a Report published in 1834. This would in turn lead to the Poor Law Amendment Act, known as the New Poor Law, ushering in a much harsher climate for the nation's paupers, especially those in the County Institutions – or workhouses.

Naturally, as a precursor to change, the Commissioners to the Inquiry sought the views of those responsible for distributing existing parish relief. As controller of 500 of Great Shelford's total acreage of 1400 – and the farmer of a further 900 acres in neighbouring parishes – Peter Grain was just such a figure.

His statements to the Commission make it plain that Farmer Grain felt the cost of parish relief keenly. Paying 10s per acre poor rate made support of those labourers 'congesting' the parish (ie those for whom there was no work – estimated by Peter Grain to number thirty families), a considerable, not to say intolerable financial burden. In practice, Grain generously provided soup for the poor and employed more men than he actually needed, so he could keep them from draining parish resources. But on the moral character of such people, Peter Grain is unsparing:

> ...*as the poor were well attended to by my father and the other occupants and owners in the parish, none would ever quit it, and they have gone on increasing, till they have become what they are now, idle, dissolute, good for nothing, and the real masters of the parish.*

Grain traces in this mass of indolents frustrating ingratitude in place of thanks for his charity. He combats head-on the notion – promoted by people like John Denson of Waterbeach – that a noble peasant lay untapped within every agricultural labourer. According to Denson a worker needed only a patch of ground to cultivate and a shovel-full of self-respect in order to raise himself and his family out of their situation. Peter Grain's experience suggested quite the opposite:

> *Sometime ago I offered a man who works for me, and is a good man enough, with a large family, an acre rent free. I said, You have a large family coming on, and if an acre will be of service to you for a garden, and to keep a pig or two, you are welcome to it. But he would not take it...He said, Thank'ye, sir, I should like it; but I should not like to give up my privilege on the parish. I said, Why, if you have an acre rent free, you must not expect the parish to allow you what it does now. Then he said, he would rather not have it.*

And now it is not only ingratitude that Peter Grain detects, rising from this underclass like steam from cattle, but arson. He is certain the culprits are close to hand.

He reports to Mr Cowell, Assistant Commissioner to the Inquiry that, '*The Burnings were generally supposed to be the acts of the lower orders in the immediate neighbourhood*'.

What's more, Grain is convinced that the identity of the Firestarter is being wilfully concealed by his fellow workers, telling Mr Cowell that

...some months before, the barns of the tithe lessee [Henry Headly] *had been destroyed by an incendiary well known, but protected by the sympathy of his fellows.*[62]

If there is one thing we can be sure of in the late Spring of 1833, it is that Peter Grain's own sympathy has long ago evaporated. He is determined to flush out this elusive Firestarter, wherever he lurks.

★

Though we have no record of it, it's possible that the first meeting of farmers we imagined taking place in the yard at Rectory Farm, was followed by another, more inclusive meeting. Other respectable members of the community would be present at this wider gathering – the vicar Henry Finch, the village tradespeople, respected elders like William Cambridge, and so on.

At either meeting, Peter Grain's pitch would be the same. In a bid to be free from the attacks that are terrorising their village, the village 'elders' have twice put their trust in outside agencies. Firstly, with the Earl of Hardwicke's help. On that occasion, Samuel Taunton of the Bow Street Public Office had been brought up from London. He'd succeeded only in arresting the pitiful pauper Joseph Ellerm. Taunton's case had been humiliatingly dismissed as baseless by the

Grand Jury – a complete waste of time and money. Then the Cambridge Magistrate Edward Serocold Pearce had intervened – or interfered, depending on your opinion. He had drawn another Bow Street Runner into the fray in the towering form of George Leadbitter, with a similarly dismal result. George Leadbitter's expenses claim for the quarter in which he visited Great Shelford amounted to £13.12s.[63] Again, a complete waste of money. And all the time, farmers' property was being destroyed. Now summer was coming. It would not just be barns that were vulnerable if this baking heat continued. Given the accelerating rate of the flare-ups, it was only a matter of time until someone – probably someone in the current meeting – was burned to a crisp in their bed. The time had come for the village to take matters into its own hands.

Here was the plan:

It must be impressed on every soul in the village, from the youngest child and humblest servant to the closest neighbour and most distant relation, that it was their express duty to report anything untoward directly to Peter Grain himself, or to fetch the village constable.

At this point Samuel Holder would have stepped forward. How long Holder had held his unenviable office is difficult to tell, but his presence in Great Shelford in 1833 suggests the villagers anticipated they might need reinforcements.

Village constables were usually unarmed – unlike Bow Street Runners – but were frequently called upon to enforce the law at local level. Holder himself been employed in Cambridge the previous year as an inspector and officer of the Mendicity Society – deployed in moving on vagrants from the streets of the city (*plus ça change*, you might conclude).[64] Now he was part of the forces bent on detecting and detaining the scourge of Great Shelford. At least he was relatively local.

The meeting perhaps concluded with a dread reminder from Peter Grain, from Samuel Holder, or perhaps more likely from the Reverend Finch, that for any prosecution to be successful, sworn testimony would be required when the case came before the Assizes. This would be hard, if the culprit turned out to be someone the witnesses knew, perhaps someone they had grown up with. But testify they must. For make no mistake, this reign of terror had to be ended. And God was on the side of justice.

All this was before the fire at Kirby & Tunwell's broke out on Thursday, the twenty-third day of that sweltering May. That would be the day when, for the first time, the shadow of suspicion finally began to edge in John Stallon's direction.

According to the account given later in court, the episode played out like this:

William Kirby shared a barn with his fellow farmer Henry Tunwell. With all the talk, not to mention evidence of a fire raiser at large, Kirby was determined not to be caught out. On the morning of the twenty third of May he turned the key in the door of his barn, keeping his mess of straw and tools safe from intruders. Only the most cunning thief lifting the key from its hook in Farmer Kirby's kitchen – where he next went to store it – could possibly get inside his barn. Finishing up his breakfast, and with the key still swinging on its hook, Kirby then went off to work in the fields, only returning to his home at five o' clock that afternoon.

Meanwhile, around midday a labourer called Allen Kifford had taken his dinner break after spending the morning digging in a field owned by Peter Grain, near to Kirby's barn. Kifford was returning to work when he paused in a close to wait for his dog who had taken off after a rabbit or hare. That was when Kifford spied John Stallon, walking down the lane toward Kirby's yard. At the same time, from a different direction, a woman came along. Stallon, seeing this woman, doubled back until she'd headed off in a different direction. Then he returned to the barn.

'I was between three and four poles from him', Kifford

would later tell the court; 'I heard him strike as if with a piece of iron or steel, I could at that time just see his head; he then came out of the close with one hand in his jacket pocket; he went to the back of the barn, and I saw him run his hand through the clay wall, but whether he put anything in I don't know...'[65]

Kifford threw something – a piece of earth or a stone – towards Stallon, and thought he might have scared him off. Except that, half an hour later, Allen Kifford looked up from the field where he was working to see smoke fogging the sky. It was coming from the direction of Kirby and Tunwell's barn. Heeding the alarm, he immediately dropped his tools and ran to get the engine – only to find John Stallon was already there. John coolly nudged Kifford aside and told him to stay quiet.

Kifford had indeed stayed quiet. Only much later that day did he tell his brother what he'd seen. He also told Mr William Headly. There were other labourers who would step up later to say they too had seen Stallon in the lanes at about the time in question. And at some point, either Kifford or William Headly passed this information on to the Constable, Samuel Holder. When Holder questioned John Stallon he found in John's possession a knife that looked as though it had been repeatedly used to draw sparks from a piece of flint. For now though, all the evidence linking John Stallon to the fire was circumstantial – the matter was allowed to rest.

This left Stallon at liberty to select his next target – one we might feel betrays extreme calculation – or a terrible, fateful, recklessness.

Perhaps John already detected the whiff of sulphur in the air. Or perhaps he had been replaying in his head some of what he'd overheard from the margins of those public meetings; the tone of outrage among the 'powers' in the village; the indignation that someone was giving them the run around; the dismissal of any notion that Great Shelford's labourers had

anything to complain about – that they were all idle ingrates.
John's next victim would be the most powerful man in the
village.

Chapter Eighteen

CROSSING THE LINE

As an invariable rule, the agricultural labourer commences his career as a weekly labourer; and, whatever his talents and industry, he must inevitably end his days as a labourer, or when unfitted through old age to continue his work, die as a pauper.

Shirley Brooks, *Letter XX*, in Alexander Mackay & Shirley Brooks, The Morning Chronicle's *Labour and the Poor: Vol VI, The Rural Districts (1849-51)*, London: Ditto Books (2020), p.403

On Wednesday May 29th John Stallon set off from the family's cottage at first light – with one thing on his mind.

This is how the *Cambridge Chronicle* assessed the impact of what followed:

Friday June the seventh, 1833.

Another Fire at Shelford – On Wednesday morning last, about five o'clock, a fire broke out in the sheep-yard upon the farm of Mr. Peter Grain, on the Green, at Great Shelford. Fortunately, this yard was detached from the various buildings, and consequently the flames could extend no further, but they were not extinguished until about one hundred loads of haulm were destroyed. There is every reason to suppose that the object of the wretched miscreant must have been the destruction of the sheep usually penned in this yard.

Perhaps. But ovicide does not really fit the picture we have of John Stallon. He seems to have harboured no hard feelings against any living thing, human or animal – with the possible exception of every farmer in the village. Less easy to swerve is the conclusion that, however much Stallon may claim his choice of targets was driven by convenience, from the distance of two centuries there is an undeniable 'completer-finisher' look to the list of those who found their property destroyed. Most of the bigger farmers in the village are there; the Headly brothers, Thomas Stacey, William Cambridge, and now Peter Grain himself, the biggest beast of them all. If it is not a political list, it is certainly an economic one, for these are among the key employers of Great Shelford's poorly paid and discontented agricultural labourers.

As far as the farmers are concerned, if the decision had already been made that the village must resolve this situation for itself, the impudence of this latest attack on Peter Grain's sheep pen gave the hunt for the arsonist a new impulse.

The next attempted fire – though it involves a notable change in fire-lighting technology – would end John Stallon's incendiary spree for ever.

★

Elizabeth Stallon feels a weight, so heavy inside her – worse than any pregnancy. It is the downward plunge of inevitable, encroaching, inescapable disaster. Trying to pinpoint the moment when she first began to feel this weight was difficult. The fire at Old Cambridge's farm, so close by, had been a shock. Her friend Sarah was alive only because she'd been shaken from her bed. Sarah had been there, on the farm, with her children, young people now, clinging to each other in fear as the engine was pumped and pumped and John ran about uncoiling the hose, passing out buckets, doing the work of three men in a battle against flames leaping from the barn. Across this mad scramble Sarah and Elizabeth's eyes had met. Had Sarah seen it then? Elizabeth had not known John would do this, how could she? That was ridiculous. How could she know Old Cambridge's farm would be John's next target?

For her to know that and not warn Sarah was unthinkable. But something passed between them, some moment of recognition, along with the shouts and the crying and the crack of beams exploding in the barn.

This new dissonance was still there in the days following, in the minute adjustments, the tiny shifts imperceptible to anyone but Elizabeth. People changing their position, drawing back, edging away as if knowing a disaster was coming and that she, and John, were somehow at the centre of it. Soon all would be engulfed in massive events, a roil of history that would swallow anyone too close to their unfortunate family.

The wonder is this weight did not cause Elizabeth to pull away from what was coming. The opposite. It drew her in, compelled her towards it so that a few days later, after the fire at Kirby's when John had come home shaken for reasons Elizabeth did not dare ask about, and again after the fire at the sheep pen on the Green when John had been so tired but so wild and for the first time for a long time talked about pigs and what a great thing that would be, to own a pig, and maybe a cow too so the children could have their milk. And he had raved that great people could be brought down it said so in the Bible and small people lifted up. She had almost said it to him then. But still Elizabeth waited.

When John was calm, in the morning, before he set off for the fields, Elizabeth asked him where he was working this week and he said, 'The Master's' and she had asked if he meant at Rectory Farm or in Henry Headly's close above the Green and he said, 'the close'. And she had finally said 'Well then. You will be near William Dean's. He should be next'.

John had held Elizabeth's gaze for the longest time. And then something changed in him. He looked to Elizabeth in that moment like a pillowcase washed in the tub – one with all the air steadily going out of it. He had glanced up the stairs to see if John Jr was awake, and then said in the smallest voice.

'Now is the time for no flare-up'.

And she had said his name, 'John', in a tone which made it clear this was something he could not deny her, but before she had barely started telling him what she had never told anyone – about what she had suffered in the fields years before – he had spoken in an even quieter and more urgent voice.

'I have been at this a long time, wife'.

And then he had picked up his coat and walked out.

For a week Elizabeth had done nothing. She and John spoke no more about William Dean, or what she had been through on his land, or about anything. And then he told her one night that the next day was his last in the close for a while and again Elizabeth said nothing.

By the next morning she'd made a decision. When John went off to work, taking John Jr with him, Elizabeth pulled the stool up beneath the shelf where she kept her treasure box. Since Sarah had told her what she'd placed in the box Elizabeth had not gone close. Perhaps it was Elizabeth herself who was superstitious. She had not wanted to release the power of the Lucifers into her family's life. Now that ship had sailed; it was time to take some control. All her disadvantages she now saw were advantages. Nobody would suspect her – they hardly even saw her. And this way, this time, John would have witnesses that he was not the culprit. This morning Elizabeth had stood on the stool and straightening as much as she was able, reached the box down and pulled off the lid.

The Lucifers were not there.

Chapter Nineteen

A RAGGED-APRONED INCENDIARIST?

It is very desirable that the labouring classes of society should be respectable and comfortable in their circumstances; that they should be able to provide themselves with decent habitation, wholesome food, and suitable raiment. The happiness of every benevolent person is advanced by observing and promoting the happiness of those around him; and in proportion as its population is thriving and contented, in that proportion is a nation secured both against invading foes, and internal discord.

Esther Hewlett, *Cottage Comforts*, 2nd Edition, London: Simpkin & Marshall, 1826, p.B

On the afternoon of June 12th 1833, John Stallon found himself doing his least favourite work. It was a gloomy, blustery day in the weeding season with a 'lazy wind' whistling through John's coat, choosing to blow through the man rather than go around. Stallon had told John Jr to stay at home after dinner. It was miserable work, hooking out weeds without disturbing the crop, a task made all the trickier by the clagginess of the soil after rain. And anyway, William Headly said he would not pay a boy for work his father was already set to. Stay home, draw out your letters.

John had not been back weeding half an hour after dinner, working alongside a red-haired labourer called Richard Jeffery, when Mr William Headly appeared and called John over. Richard had looked askance, but John gave him the smallest shrug – I've no idea – before obediently approaching the farmer, his head bowed slightly in the expected submissive manner. Had John seen anyone pass between Tom Kefford's house (next door) and Maris's gate, when he came back from dinner? John shook his head, but then recalled he had seen a boy.

'I just saw Tom Kefford's lad, and young John Dean, Mr William Dean's lad, the young Master – though come to think of it, that may have been earlier, this morning'.

Mr William Headly pursed his lips, the nostrils of his long old nose flaring. He was used to this kind of obfustication from labourers – though not usually this one. He sent John back to his work.

'Something's up then', Richard Jeffrey said when John got back to his row.

'Looks like', said John, glancing towards the barn. 'Maybe someone's robbed Dean's place'.

A short time later, just as John and Richard were quietly wondering to each other how soon they would be allowed to finish and agreeing they could use a drink on the way home, William Headly returned to the field accompanied by a Magistrate, the Revd Musgrave, and John was arrested.

★

In the case of attempted arson at Mr William Dean's barn, a small ball of blue-patterned rags, singed by fire, lies at the centre. These burning rags had allegedly been tossed into William Dean's barn just below the roof.

The barn itself was built of posts and planks with straw as a thatch laid on top. The rag ball allegedly lay a foot below the roof smouldering in the straw, till the smoke was seen by William Dean and his son John. The two men reached into the barn to grab handfuls of smoking straw, pulling it out into the yard to save the barn. When the straw fell out, the rags came too.

What we conclude about this ball of rags, lying on the yard at Farmer Dean's – where it came from, and who lodged it in the outhouse – determines who we think was responsible for this latest fire – and whether John Stallon's arrest and subsequent trial were justified.

Four possibilities – at least four – are worth exploring.

The first, and perhaps the most far-fetched possibility – but also, a very seductive one, as all conspiracy theories are – is that John Stallon's guilt as the Shelford Arsonist had already been decided by the more senior farmers. The business at Kirby and Tunwell's barn, John Stallon's eagerness in manning the engine and collecting his money, had finally dismantled the Big Four's good opinion of him. Even in Henry Headly's heart, something hardened. But as the Reverend Pearce had earlier noted, believing you have identified a culprit and proving it are two separate things. Somehow, an irrefutable link was needed between the man and his mayhem. How ever that was discovered – or created – it had to be done for the good of the village.

As would be attested at the trial, the ball of rags, once 'found', passed from hand to hand. It also passed up the chain of command. Mr William Dean gives it to his wife Sarah; she gives it to Mr William Headly; he, 'after some time', which seems to mean the next day, June 13th, passes it to Mr Grain.

That Thursday morning, Peter Grain inspects the patterned rags and 'in consequence of some information' goes directly to the house of Sarah Cambridge. There, miraculously, he finds that pieces of material in her workbasket match the pattern of the rags exactly. With something like astonishment, Sarah Cambridge says she gave some of the material to her friend, Elizabeth, wife of John Stallon. Peter Grain crosses the road – now with Samuel Holder the Constable in tow. In the absence of John Stallon (he is being questioned by the Magistrate), the two search the tenement where the Stallons live with their two small sons. Grain and Holder find inside that dark, cramped cottage not only matching rags in Elizabeth's workbasket, but two aprons made from identical material, hanging by the stove. Elizabeth confirms that Sarah Cambridge gave her an old dress, which she has cut up – so what?

The same day, while all this is happening, William Dean reinspects the straw he and his son pulled out of the outhouse the day before and recovers two matches which have somehow survived the incident unignited. These matches, Mr Dean concludes, must have fallen from the ball of rags. The rags and the matches together constitute a primitive incendiary device. When this information is conveyed to Peter Grain the case against John Stallon is, as surely as the straw in William Dean's outhouse, cut and dried.

To those of a sceptical mind, the vagueness of the phrase used by Peter Grain to explain how the material led him to visit Mrs Cambridge's house is interesting: '*in consequence of some information*' is, in this view, a major leap, conveniently bridged.

In addition, it does seem strange that John Stallon would change his method – or at least the pyrotechnical part of it – so late in his career as incendiary.

Lucifer matches had been readily available to anyone in England with a small amount of cash for at least three years by this time. John Archer in his book *A Flash and a Scare*, directly links the commercial availability of Lucifers to the spate of incendiarism associated with the Swing Riots of 1830.[66] Yet the sound of metal striking against something hard, and the knife that was found in Stallon's possession after the fire at Kirby and Tunwell's barn – the knife showing signs of being used in striking flint – were offered as evidence against John in the second charge he faced in the trial – the blazing of the barn at Kirby and Tunwell's. Is it likely that John, knowing that suspicion was growing after that earlier brush with discovery would now take the extra risk of carrying matches to work with him?

But perhaps the speed of striking a match suddenly seemed worth the extra risk. Perhaps what John had learned from that earlier, narrow escape, was that it was foolish to hang around trying to get a spark from his tinderbox when a match could set a blaze much faster. Having placed those Lucifers in his house just a few chapters ago – albeit via Sarah Cambridge's kind intentions – I have obviously placed temptation in his path.

And again, going back to the ball of rags in Peter Grain's hand, perhaps the information in Mr Grain's ear that became of such consequence by linking the rags to Mrs Cambridge, simply came from a random act of recognition on the part of Mrs Dean; perhaps she had seen Sarah Cambridge (the younger Sarah Cambridge) walking by her house in a dress of just that material the previous summer when that Sarah, the younger Sarah Cambridge, was going to visit her sister-in-law (the older Sarah Cambridge) whose school was just along the road from the Dean's place, in High Green.

Despite the allure of a village-wide conspiracy to entrap John Stallon, it seems unlikely. At the trial that followed, all these people would give their accounts on oath. These were god-fearing people. Probably, the tracing of the material, while certainly fortuitous, correctly ties the fire to John Stallon's household.

This leads us, unfortunately, to consider a second alternative to John Stallon's guilt. A suggestion that seems both wild and unlikely; the real arsonist on this occasion at least may not have been John Stallon. It may have been Elizabeth, his wife.

I have, as you are aware, made this wild suggestion seem a tiny bit less wild, by suggesting that Elizabeth was keen to see Mr Dean's barn targeted – so much so that, in my account, she suggests it to her husband; he, Dean, should be next. Moreover, I've hinted that someone, not necessarily Mr Dean himself but someone connected to his farm has misused Elizabeth, sexually, sometime in the past at harvest time. In the story as I have told it, a justifiable pool of fury is rising in Elizabeth and surging toward revenge. I have even had her reaching for the matches.

There is not a shred of evidence for any of this supposition, except that such experiences were not uncommon for women working the land at this time. But even this rather desperate arguing from silence is irrelevant.

Whatever motive we might falsely – or truthfully – attribute to Elizabeth, we are forced to consider the possibility that she may have set the fire at William Dean's, for one simple reason. John himself said she did it.

After John's arrest and detainment in Cambridge Castle, he and Elizabeth were questioned by the Magistrate, a man called Musgrave. On the second day, John, still protesting his innocence, was questioned by the Revd Musgrave on two further occasions. We might conclude that this could not be as intimidating an experience as that suffered by Robert Elborne and William Shearing at the hands of George Leadbitter and the Revd Edward Serocold Pearce, let alone as harrowing as Samuel Taunton's interrogation of Joseph Ellerm. But still, after a night in the cells of the County Gaol, the terror to come if he was found guilty would not be lost on John Stallon.

With a panic rising in his head as powerful as that sickening weight in poor Elizabeth's stomach, John begins to check his avenues of escape. He begins to cast suspicion on anyone he can think of.

The first person he attempts to implicate is a fellow labourer, Foxey Deans. Coming home one day John found Foxey leaning over from Mr Grain's close that ran alongside *Woodlands* cottage. He was pulling a piece of blue cloth from the dung heap in Stallon's yard. John had offered to supply Foxey with another piece of the same cloth, if he wanted it, but was curious to know what it was for. Foxey had – according to John – assured Stallon that in a couple of days he would find out.

In the second interview with Musgrave, John threw the muck even closer to home. When he arrived home for dinner at 1pm on the day of the fire, Elizabeth had, John said, expressed surprise. 'I didn't expect you to be home so soon', she said. 'I thought you would have been stopped on the road. I made a ball with rags, matches and tinder and put it in Dean's place. I thought it would have broken out by now'. John claimed he replied that she had 'made a pretty thing of it' but said no more.

Suppose for a moment that John's claim to be innocent is true; is it possible that Elizabeth Stallon is guilty?

One person present at the County Gaol when John delivered his tale clearly thought it a ridiculous proposition. He set about collecting the evidence to prove it.

Chapter Twenty

MR ORRIDGE INVESTIGATES

With axe at root he felled thee to the ground
And barked of freedom...
John Clare, *The Fallen Elm*

Prisons in Britain in the nineteenth century were run largely as private businesses. The board of directors employed a governor – elected by the county's magistrates – and paid him an annual salary. Robert Orridge held the post of Governor of the Cambridge County Gaol for a total of thirty years. This was a time of huge change at the prison. The old castle keep was pulled down, and in its place a purpose-built new gaol established. Building on the ideas of reformers like John Howard, the new design by George Byfield featured an octagonal house for the governor from which radiated four wings, each split longitudinally to accommodate two classes of prisoner in each wing. Upstairs were sleeping rooms, downstairs day rooms. Between the wings were exercise yards.

On the first floor of the Governor's house, in addition to his own office and further rooms available to the magistrates, there was a light and airy chaplaincy – though even this was divided into ten parts to keep the different grades (and genders) of prisoner apart. As in the world outside the prison, the grading of persons was a feature. If you were in the debtor's section for example, there was accommodation for two classes of inmate: Masters, and Commoners. In the Masters' debtor section you could, if you had the means, choose what furnishings to add to your iron bedstead. If you were in the Commoners' section you made do with a straw mattress, two blankets and a coverlet. [67]

Conditions for those on criminal charges were even less salubrious than this. Public executions still followed virtually every session of the biannual Assizes; as we learned from Joseph Ellerm's incarceration, detainment on a charge of arson was no picnic.

Like many trades and professions at the time, the responsibility of running prisons tended to run in families. Robert Orridge's brother John Orridge held the equivalent post at the prison in Bury St Edmunds, concurrent with Robert's term of office in Cambridge. Nor were the rewards of the post insubstantial. When Robert retires in just three years' time – he will (like the Earl of Hardwicke) pass his title on to a nephew (in this case, his brother John's son, Charles. Up till now, Charles Orridge had worked as a chemist; even positions in a family business took time to become available).[68] Once retired from his post, Robert will live the life of a gentlemen, for the salary he has received – £200 per annum – allows him to declare himself in the 1841 census a man of independent means. He will still maintain an interest in penal affairs, but this will be as a paid-up member of the Town of Cambridge Association whose AGM and dinner took place each June at the *Wrestler's Inn* in Petty Cury, that famously narrow street in the centre of Cambridge. The society's founding objectives might seem to us similarly narrow, aiming to promote the 'prosecution of Felons and Thieves of every denomination'. [69] But that is all three years hence; for now, Robert Orridge is governor of the County Gaol, a man committed to his role, and determined to play his part in securing the conviction (and saving the soul) of the Shelford Arsonist. For the role of prison governor – then as now – included not only responsibility for the secure imprisonment of inmates, but a duty to pursue their welfare. Mr Orridge (whether John at Bury or Robert at Cambridge) frequently acted as confessor, sometimes working in shifts with the prison chaplains. Their aim is to persuade prisoners to make confession, especially in cases of capital crimes.

For some days now Robert has been much troubled by the case of John Stallon. He has listened to Stallon's protestations of innocence without surprise. Experience has taught him such claims are commonplace when suspects realise their lives might stand forfeit for their crimes. But for a man to implicate his wife was extraordinary. Seeing Elizabeth Stallon refute any accusation of guilt when called before the magistrate, and noting her tiny stature, Robert Orridge determines to do what he can to defend the woman – and to help John Stallon save his eternal soul by eventually admitting his guilt.

Rising early, Orridge tells his manservant to bring around his carriage.

One of the downsides of living over the shop – or in this case, at the centre of a prison – is that the world easily shrinks to the confines of what one can see from a window. Despite having served at the prison for twenty-seven years by this time, Robert Orridge has never visited Great Shelford. Happily, his servant, who has brought the gig alongside the governor's house, is on hand to supply the necessary intelligence; the village is a medium-sized, not especially friendly place, about five miles from Cambridge.

The gig sets off, with Mr Orridge wondering how, when he gets to this village, he should best present himself. He decides in fact, to locate John Stallon's cottage indirectly. First, he goes to the farm of William Cambridge. Orridge has had some dealings with the Cambridge family in the past. While he does not anticipate a euphoric response to the Governor of the County Gaol appearing on the doorstep, he knows he can rely on Old Cambridge's recognition of him. Mr Orridge was once a help in time of need to William Cambridge: he is hopeful that the kindness will be returned.

He finds Old Cambridge not in the best of health, and his wife Hannah not much better. Their daughter-in-law, Sarah, seems to run the house. When Orridge tells her whom he is seeking, her jaw noticeably tightens. At William's prompting, Sarah nods toward the big house opposite. It's the little cottage behind there, she says.

Mr Orridge thanks her, and walks back down the farm track, gesturing to his man to follow with the gig. He wants to take a look at the barn they trundled past on the way to the farmhouse. Blackened and all but destroyed by fire, the ruin fills Robert's nostrils with the stench of burned and dampened haulm. Little has been done to clear it up. Whoever does the farmwork once done by Old Cambridge must be waiting for the old man's insurance pay-out before organising the building of a new barn. They'd better get a move on, with harvest round the corner.

Arriving at the cottage opposite, Mr Orridge knocks on the door and removes his hat while stepping back a little from the threshold. He catches a glimpse of someone in the upstairs window of the neighbouring tenement, but then the downstairs door of this cottage is opened, and the tiny figure of Elizabeth Stallon somehow fills the space.

'Mrs Stallion, do you know me?', he says.

Elizabeth's eyes flick sideways, running back down the path Orridge has walked up. Then they fix back on him.

'I do, Mr Orridge'.

'I'm sorry I have no great news of John. He is well, tolerably'.

Elizabeth nods in thanks for this titbit of kindness, and waits.

'I wonder if I might come inside to talk to you'.

She says nothing, but backs away into the house, leaving the door open.

As soon as he is in the house, Orridge realises he has made this woman conscious of her vulnerability. In the corner is a cot with a shape beneath a pile of blankets.

'Perhaps there's a friend who could watch the child, or sit

with you while we have a private conversation?', he asks.

'I'll take him'.

Orridge is at first unsure where this third voice has come from, but now he sees that the woman from the window next door has appeared in the doorway.

'Thank you', says Orridge, 'that would be helpful, Mrs…'

'I'm the neighbour', says Sarah Walker, and pushes past the man of some importance, to pick up the child.

'Could you stay…please', says Orridge.

The women exchange a glance. Sarah Walker's role as chaperone agreed, Mr Orridge continues.

'Mrs Stallion, I must make an unusual request. May I take a measurement of your height?'.

Elizabeth gives him a long look.

'Will it help John?' she says at last.

'It may help your family, Mrs Stallion'.

Elizabeth wraps her arms around herself but does not say 'no'.

'Perhaps you would stand against the wall. Do you have such a thing as a book, I might borrow?'

Elizabeth fetches John's book from its place on the shelf. Robert Orridge nods to himself in recognition. *Robinson Crusoe.*

Now Elizabeth stands with her back to the wall and looks at him, waiting for the ordeal to begin.

'Please, stretch your body to its tallest self, Mrs Stallion', says Orridge and produces from his pocket the tape measure he has borrowed from William Calcraft. Despite being, he hopes, a man of science, it flickers across Robert Orridge's thoughts that the only time he has seen Calcraft the prison executioner using the measure is in preparing the length of the drop for some poor wretch's dispatch. He pushes that thought aside. He is here not to take a life, but hopefully, with God's help, to save it. Or in any case to save a soul, albeit indirectly.

Being as bent as she is, Elizabeth Stallon cannot press both her back and her head against the wall at the same time. It will have to be the back, and that will have to do. Standing to one side of Elizabeth, Orridge lays *Robinson Crusoe* firmly across the top of her head, treads the end of the measure to the floor, and reads off the mark against the lower edge of the book, keeping the yellowing tape as straight as he can.

Just shy of four feet.

'Now…', says Orridge, placing the book back upon a chair and making a note in a tiny daybook with a stub of pencil.

'That's good. Now…', he says again, '…can I ask you Mrs Stallion to stretch your hand above your head and reach to your full… Yes, that's best, face the wall like that and reach high. Hold still, if you can…'

'Ssssssssh', says Sarah Walker behind him, and begins to coo the waking child, whose name Orridge will one day be told by its father is William, after a brother who died in the most violent of circumstances.

Orridge reads off the measure where it touches the tip of Elizabeth Stallon's longest finger. 5' 7".

'Ha' he says, and seems pleased, adding these figures to the note in his little red book.

'Thank you, Mrs Stallion'.

And Robert Orridge disappears from the cottage to make his next, vital measurement.

Chapter Twenty-One

THE ONLY POSSIBLE CONCLUSION

I'm John Clare now. I was Byron and Shakespeare formerly. At different times you know I'm different people – that is the same person with different names.

John Clare, to a visitor at the Northampton asylum, in Merryn and Raymond Williams, ed. *John Clare: Selected Poetry and Prose*, London: Methuen English Texts (1986), Introduction, p.19.

The link between the ball of rags and John Stallon's home is sound.

If there is no village-wide conspiracy; if Stallon himself is innocent (as he claims) and Elizabeth, whatever her desires, is physically incapable of planting the device in the roof of the barn, (as Robert Orridge is determined to demonstrate), there is one last possibility we must consider. Only one other person in the Stallon household has regular access to Elizabeth's rag bag and could have been in the area of Deans' farm on the day of the fire. That person is baby William's brother and John and Elizabeth's eldest son, John Stallon Jr.

At the time of this final fire John Junior was nine years old and two months. We have imagined him to be at least as tall as his diminutive mother. This is entirely possible. The average height of nine-year-old boys in Britain in 1836 was three feet and eleven inches.[70] There is nothing in any of the very brief mentions of the Stallon boys as children or as men to suggest they inherited their mother's restricted growth. We have had John Jr working in the fields, especially at harvest, as many boys of his age and time, did. We have also had him tearing up cloth from his mother's rag bag into bandage-like strips. Again, we have no evidence that John Jr ever did this – but it is hardly impossible.

Bandages? Or strips for a ball of rag? If the latter, was John Jr aiding and abetting his father, or aping him?

Had John Junior in fact overheard the discussion we imagined between his parents – about the firing of William Deans' farm? Had he concluded that if his father refused to defend his mother's honour, he would have to step up?

We have also suggested there were Lucifers in the house, and that John Junior had opportunity to take them. Again, neither is impossible, so let's entertain them as facts, at least for now.

Tiny details from the day of the fire now scream for attention.

One of the additional bits of information that was used to implicate John Stallon, was that he was seen loitering in the area of William Dean's outhouse when he returned from his dinner, about forty minutes before the 'fire' was discovered. John Dean saw him and thought Stallon Snr was acting suspiciously. Sarah Dean also saw him while she was out feeding her turkeys – but she thought he looked confused.

John, when first asked by William Headly if he had seen anyone pass that way, at first said 'no'. Then he corrected himself; he had seen a lad in the lane – Tom Kefford's boy – besides young Master Dean. This is all as it is in the *Cambridge Chronicle*'s transcript of the court case.

But was it really Kefford's son John saw, or another lad – a boy he had told to stay at home, who he must protect at all costs? Was it a fleeting glimpse of his own son in the lane that had thrown John into the confusion that Sarah Dean detected on the day of the fire?

Compared with John Junior's life, neither John's life, nor Elizabeth's mattered much. The couple had waited a long time for a child to survive. Is that why John tried to implicate his wife? Had John become so panicked after a night at Cambridge Castle that he had not yet realised the obvious?

All he had to do to keep suspicion from falling on John Jr was to stay silent. Or better still admit the charge himself.

We might ask whether a boy barely four feet tall was any more capable of planting the rag-ball than his mother. True, he wasn't crooked like her. And he was fit. Perhaps he climbed up the wall of the outhouse. Or could the ball have been thrown? Mr Orridge on his way back to Cambridge, measures the height of the opening in William Dean's barn at 7' – and marks this, too, in his little red book. In Orridge's eyes (and later, the eyes of the court) this closes the case against Elizabeth. Clearly, women were not thought capable of anything as athletic as throwing – Elizabeth especially so. Throwing the device might, by contrast, be John Junior's best bet. This could explain why it burned so poorly, the trailing end of the rag, reduced to a smoulder by its journey through the air.

Odd though, that the would-be arsonist was seen by no one else, apart from his half-glimpsing father. As the description of the barn and the place where the rag ball entered shows, John Jr-the-Arsonist must have been a brilliant shot – and his brilliance was untutored. It's unlikely he'd had much practice hurling a fireball.

As no less an authority on crime-solving than Sir Arthur Conan Doyle once put it,: When all other possible explanations have been dismissed, what is left, however improbable, or, as we might say, however regrettable, is the truth. By the standards of our time, the evidence against John Stallon on the charge of attempting to fire William Dean's barn looks circumstantial at best; by the standards of the day, it is conclusive.

As we have seen, Stallon was certainly no stranger to fire-raising. And in the way he behaved once arrested, John certainly did not help himself. Flinging out first one far-fetched accusation, following it with another – these look like the actions of a guilty, if desperate, individual. A man with no great plan, who was no great builder of alliances – and a fritterer-away of whatever benevolent relationships life had given him. John was also subject to the short-termism of anyone struggling to put food on the table. Through his tactical skill, John Stallon, Arsonist, had a very good run. But he was no strategist; his run had reached its end.

To those who prosecuted him for his crimes, Stallon's implication of his wife merely confirmed his wickedness, adding cowardice and betrayal to his other, devilish impulses.

The Rev Musgrave had little hesitation in committing him to stand trial at the Summer Assizes in a little over a month's time.

The farmers of Great Shelford, unlike poor, humiliated Elizabeth Stallon, could at last look to the future with some satisfaction. They had succeeded where the much-vaunted officers of the Bow Street Public Office had palpably failed. They had finally got their man.

Meanwhile, news of the arrest of the Shelford Arsonist – a previously trusted labourer named John Stallon – began its journey into the wider world.

BOOK FOUR

HARVEST

Chapter Twenty-Two

PURE DIABOLICAL REVENGE.

The Summer, like a stranger comes,
I pause — and hardly know her face.
John Clare, *On Leaving the Cottage of my Birth.*

News that a man has been arrested for the crimes of the Shelford Arsonist flies around the country. It travels in the form of syndicated stories that begin in the newspapers of East Anglia and are published wherever relations between farmers and their troublesome workers have resonance.

This is a great era for newspapers. The first steam presses are transforming the printing industry and even local papers publish huge wads of news in tiny type. Twelve column spreads relate events both local and national, from debates in Parliament to tragic suicides and news of charity dinners — all of life is here. News of the latest arrest in the case of the Shelford Arsonist provides great copy.

Huntingdon, Bedford and Peterborough Gazette; Saturday, 15 June, 1833:

The Shelford Fires. — We have reason to believe that the author or one of the authors of this series of crimes has been discovered. On Wednesday afternoon last, about three, Mr William Dean, farmer of that place, observed some smoke issuing from a stack; he immediately threw some water on it, and succeeded in extinguishing it, and we understand before it entirely consumed the combustible articles with which the fire was communicated. In consequence of some strong suspicion, a man of the name of John Stallion was apprehended and has undergone several examinations, the particulars of which have not transpired. He is committed for further examination.

The following week, there is an update courtesy of the *Cambridge Chronicle*, Friday 21 June, 1833…

COMMITMENTS TO THE CASTLE: John Stallion, (by the Rev. Thos. Musgrave,) charged with having wilfully and maliciously set on fire a cart shed at Great Shelford in the occupation of William Deans, on Wednesday the 12th instant.

While the news flies around the region and beyond, John Stallon remains in Cambridge County Gaol, stubbornly maintaining his innocence.

Avid readers of newsprint don't have to wait too long for the next development. At the beginning of August, the Summer Assizes physically arrive in Cambridge. With great pageantry the assigned Judges are welcomed to the city. Cambridge is just one stop on the judges' twice-yearly circuit around the country, mopping up serious cases that are too weighty for the Quarterly Sessions. Serious crime in the county must wait for settlement by a Grand Jury under the supervision of a senior judge – and now that moment has arrived.

Once welcomed to Cambridge, the judges declare the Commission of Assizes open – usually on Monday afternoon of the chosen week. They then sit down to a good dinner. The following day, the judges attend a divine service at Great St Mary's Church in the centre of Cambridge, before processing to Shire House. There they divide themselves between the two courts. One judge addresses the *Nisi Prius* cases – civil cases headed for the London courts unless settled locally. The second judge settles into his significantly more onerous seat in the Crown Court. He customarily gives a short address on some aspect of penal affairs, before opening accounts on the county's criminal cases. And so, by midday on Tuesday of the week of the Assizes, the barrage of trials – which may go on for the whole week – has begun its inexorable roll. [71]

The case of the Shelford Arsonist, which takes place in the

crown court on Weds 2 August, 1833 is as they say, keenly anticipated. John Stallon, firestarter, is top of the bill.

In fact, there is something processional about the way this case is conducted, as the *Cambridge Chronicle*'s account reveals.

Judge Littledale calls on a Mr Andrews to conduct the case for the prosecution. He begins by calling the prosecutor or alleged victim, Mr William Dean, poulterer. He, his wife Sarah Dean, Mr William Headly, and Mr Peter Grain each rise in turn to give their accounts of the ball of blue rags, and Mr Grain explains its tracing to the house of Sarah Cambridge, and further, to her workbasket. Sarah Cambridge is called next. Whether she fixes her eyes on those of her friend in the public gallery – or avoids them – Sarah testifies that she passed on pieces of just that material to the prisoner's wife and was therefore able to supply two identical samples to the Constable. Mr Holder confirms that he received the rags from Mrs Cambridge, and matched them to rags found in the Stallon's home. Both were identical to those used in the fireball.

Having established the main case, Mr Andrews sets about discrediting John Stallon's two alternative accounts of how Mr Dean's barn was fired. First, he brings Foxey Deans to the stand. Foxey – or William, to give him his proper name – refutes John's story about the rag plucked from the dung heap, swearing he has never been near John Stallon's yard. He is backed up by another labourer, John Turner, who solemnly declares that on the day of the fire he had worked with Foxey Deans washing sheep at the sheep pen on the green at Great Shelford. They were together, working side by side, all day from early morning till late afternoon. Foxey Dean's alibi is fast.

One story dismissed, Mr Andrews turns to the second. He calls the Governor of Cambridge County Gaol, Mr Robert Orridge. Mr Orridge explains that having seen 'Mrs Stallion' before the magistrate, and noting her very small and crooked form, he measured her. Her height was a little below four feet, and her maximum reach, he declares, is 5'7". This falls well short of the breach in the outhouse through which the rag ball was pushed – which he measured at perhaps two inches short of seven feet.

The case set out – and rival narratives dismissed – the prosecution case is clear. Now John Stallon raises himself from his torpor, digs deep, and makes an impassioned plea for his life. As the *Huntingdon, Bedford and Peterborough Gazette* demonstrates, he makes a surprisingly good orator:

> *The prisoner spoke long and loudly in his defence. His lamentation, his agonized feelings, and his protestations of innocence were extremely pathetic, although his expressions at times were incoherent. "I am as innocent", he cried, "of the offence of which I am charged, as our blessed Saviour who perished for the wickedness of man; as innocent as the babe that suckles at its mother's breast; as innocent as the Judge that sits before me; may he live many years, and I no more fear facing my heavenly Judge of the crime which I am charged with than standing before my earthly Judge". His supplications to the jury for mercy were numerous, and he begged of them to weigh his case in their minds as maturely as possible.*[72]

The prisoner's energy spent, the Judge too instructs the jury to consider their verdict with care. They should not be swayed by the seriousness of the case (and its penalty). Nor should they be influenced by anything they have heard outside the court.

In fact, the Grand Jury – consisting (as all juries did) of 'gentleman of good standing in the county' – wastes little time in returning its verdict. Fifteen minutes after retiring to confer, the court is reconvened, and the Grand Jury declares its verdict. The prisoner, John Stallon, is guilty. The court then turns its attention to the second case on which the prisoner has been indicted, the torching of Kirby and Tunwell's barn.

Again, the verdict is 'guilty'.

Justice Littledale dons the black cap, and offers the following observations, and the final, dreadful sentence:

Prisoner at the bar, John Stallan, you have been convicted, after a fair and impartial trial, of having unlawfully, and feloniously set fire to an outbuilding belonging to William Deans. The jury in my mind have come to a very proper conclusion; and upon that verdict I shall proceed to pass sentence upon you for although you have also been convicted of a second similar offence, I shall now make no remark upon that. The Legislature has very properly fixed the punishment of death upon such offences as yours, for not only was property destroyed, and on some occasions to a great extent, but the lives of individuals frequently placed in imminent peril; it is also a species of crime against which there is scarcely any protection. If a person is attacked by robbers he may find means to defend himself, but in such cases as the present there is hardly any escape, and persons committing them must be actuated by feelings of the very worst description. In offences of robbery or personal attacks parties may plead necessity or previous injury as a reason for their commission; in such instances as the present there can be no such excuse, the motives which would instigate the perpetration of those crimes of which you have been convicted, must arise from pure diabolical revenge, and therefore it is that the Legislature is always slow to remit any part of the sentence, and most certainly, on the present occasion, I cannot hold out to you the slightest hopes of any mitigation. I am afraid that your mind is but ill prepared for that awful change which awaits you; take therefore, I earnestly entreat you, that spiritual advice which will be afforded you in the gaol, and fervently seek that mercy at the hands of your Almighty Redeemer, which cannot be afforded you in this world. It only remains for me to order that you be taken hence to the place from whence you came, that you there be hanged by the neck until you are dead, and may the Lord have mercy upon your soul.

John's motives – despite his pleas – are condemned as '*pure diabolical revenge*', though for what is not made clear. Still, this phrase will fly around the country, the transcript appearing in full in many local 'papers – the better to tee-up accounts of the execution to come.

But wait.

Almost immediately Robert Orridge – who has functioned on the day of the trial as both a witness and gaoler – is instructed to hold off from carrying out the judge's sentence. John Stallon has received a stay of execution.

Chapter Twenty-Three

FRIENDS IN NEED

'You cannot expect mercy this side of the grave – you must *not expect it; the gates of mercy are forever closed'.*

Baron Vaughan, Judge, passing sentence of death on Reader, Turner & Howard in March 1830. *Huntingdon, Bedford & Peterborough Gazette* – Saturday 20 March 1830

The staying of an execution in England at this time often suggests the exciting – not to say, gratifying – possibility that the prisoner will be saved by a petition for clemency.

We have seen this in the case of the almost-murder of Henry Thurnall of Whittlesford at the hands of three local labourers. Sentenced to be hanged, the fate of Ephraim Lichfield and John Nunn and Simeon Nunn-the-younger did for a while, hang in the balance. Only the strenuous efforts of the prosecutor – Henry Thurnall – and his colleagues at Nash & Wedd (solicitors) of Royston, rallied the great and good of the village of Whittlesford to prise mercy from the cold hands of Viscount Melbourne, the Home Secretary (and future Prime Minister). The sentence was commuted. Ephraim and John would be imprisoned for life with hard labour, and young Simeon was transported; a mean kind of mercy perhaps, but all three would be thankful.[73]

Even in Great Shelford's own recent past, villagers had clubbed together in a similar manner to rescue one of their own from disaster. This is a case that involves several characters we have already met.

In 1827 a man named Thomas Cambridge – youngest son of William Cambridge, and husband to Sarah Cambridge (the

younger) – was convicted of stealing a fish. Found guilty, he
found himself subject to the only sentence the law at the time
allowed for this crime – transportation for seven years.

In the face of this draconian sentence, the powers of the
village tripped into action. The case for mitigation, as their
petition put it, was this: Thomas' father William had raised
four other children very respectably. What's more, the father
was of great age – seventy-four years – and was in poor health.
The son – though listed at the time as a miller rather than
a farmer or carpenter (and regarded by his prison guards as
'*a loose character*') – was needed to take on his father's affairs.
Furthermore, the petition protested, the sentence passed
had since been superceded by a more lenient punishment
which the judge, if he had been able to call on it, would have
applied in this case. Finally, it was the petition's claim that
the defendant (despite being aged thirty at the time of the
offence) stole the large carp in question under the influence
of an older man of 'bad character'.

The petition was signed not only by the prosecutor or
victim William Foster – the man from the nearby village of
Hauxton whose pond had been raided – but also by the vicar
of the parish, Rev. Henry Finch, and eighteen prominent
villagers from Great Shelford. Accordingly, the signatures
which follow the petition include in addition to the above,
some very familiar figures – Thomas Stacey, Henry Headly
and Peter Grain:

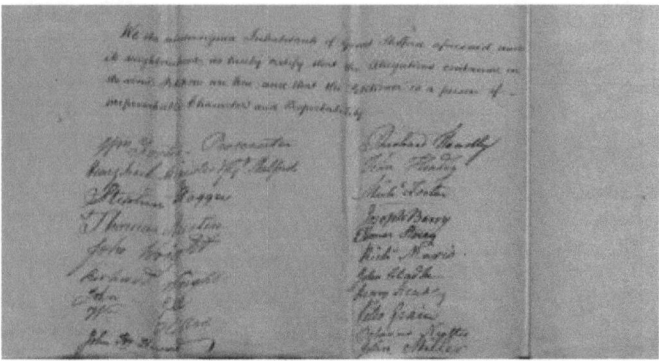

The last of Shelford's Big Four, William Headly, was clearly out of town on the day the petition came around. Nonetheless, the plea – backed up by no fewer than three letters of support from a local peer, Lord Godolphin Osborne – was successful. Thomas Cambridge's sentence was commuted to one year in prison with hard labour. [74]

The 1841 census reveals that Thomas Cambridge later returned safely to the village – but not to share a house with his wife Sarah and their children. Instead, he is living with a woman called Ann. She is the same age as Thomas, while his occupation is listed as 'Navy P' – meaning royal navy pensioner. It seems Thomas traded his prison sentence for service at sea – and never quite returned to harbour.

Was this the reason for the delay in hanging John Stallon? Were John and Elizabeth's neighbours busily organising a petition against his execution?

Apparently not. In fact, the opposite is true.

Shortly after John's conviction and sentence, the following letter appears in *The Morning Post, Monday 19 August*. It is signed, rather cynically, A. Farmer.

Sir I beg to call your attention and that of your numerous readers to a paragraph that has appeared in most of the Papers (extracted from the 'Cambridge Chronicle'*) stating that John Stallan, an incendiary who is under conviction and sentence of death, had confessed to being accessory to* twelve fires, nine *of which had caused the destruction of the buildings, and that his sole object for doing so was to receive the paltry reward of 6s 6d as an assistant at the engines. This monster fired the premises* of his own master *five times!! To this man our enlightened rulers, with that care for the lives and property of His MAJESTY's subjects which has ever distinguished them, have granted a respite to the 7ᵗʰ of December which every one knows is the same thing with a reprieve from the capital punishment.*

Now, Sir, I am no advocate for the indiscriminate infliction of the last punishment in all the cases of felony for which our Legislature has adjudged it, but I do think a worse selection of an individual for mercy

could not have been made, unless there be some very strong grounds
for it which have not met the public eye; and what those grounds
are every British subject who has any property to lose has a right to
demand from the Government who propose to save from his well-
merited punishment a fiend like this John Stallon...

Mr A. Farmer need not have worried. The delay in carrying
out the dread sentence against 'the monster' & 'fiend' John
Stallon was a purely technical one. On the 17th of August –
the day originally set for the execution – the following entry
had appeared in the *Cambridge Independent Press*, attempting to
explain the legal point at issue:

This convict, who was to have been executed to-day has been
respited until Saturday, the 7th of December and it is probable that
his execution may not take place till after the next Lent Assizes. The
circumstances are these: Stallan was convicted on two distinct offences,
but sentence was only passed upon him on one conviction. In that
indictment he was charged with having set fire to an out-house; whereas
the evidence proved that he set fire to a cart-shed; and an argument has
been raised on the part of the prisoner that the evidence did not sustain
the indictment, inasmuch as the cart-shed being an unenclosed building
cannot be regarded as a house or out-house; and Mr Justice Littledale,
who tried the prisoner, has deemed the objection of sufficient weight
to induce him to stay execution until the opinion of the Judges can be
taking on the point; but this cannot be done until Michaelmas term,
which does not commence till November...

The new date set for Stallon's hanging – December the 7th
– meant the scope for an intervention aimed at commuting
his sentence was now a full three months – plenty of time for
friends and neighbours to get over their fury, collect signatures
and appeal to the Home Secretary for clemency for a man
who, unlike the attackers of Henry Thurnall, had injured no
one.

Alas, if the village of Great Shelford was united in speaking out at the trial, it was also united now in maintaining a shattering silence. No one it seems wished, or dared, to speak up for the man they had until recently regarded as one of their own. No matter that Stallon had a wife and two young children, all of whom would, if he was taken from them, face a very uncertain future. Even Peter Grain, averse as he was to yet more villagers becoming dependent on the charity of the parish, could find no reason in his head or heart to challenge the sentence.

Perhaps it is not surprising. At the trial, John had declared to the Judge that he had no witnesses to call, either for character or for any other purpose. He was not wrong.

With the harvest now past, the last days, weeks and months of John Stallon's life on earth were beginning to tick by.

For Shelford's Big Four however, events are picking up. With the resolution of the incendiary problem, they can finally focus on another, long held vision. On Friday 27 September 1833, the following appears on the front page of the *Cambridge Chronicle and Journal:*

GREAT SHELFORD
Notice is hereby given, that APPLICATION is intended to be made in the next Session of Parliament, for leave to bring in a BILL for DIVIDING, ALLOTTING, and INCLOSING the Open and Common Fields, Commons, Commonable Lands and Waste Grounds in the parish of GREAT SHELFORD, in the county of Cambridge...

If a petition to save John Stallon never got off the ground, this may be part of the reason: the attention of the farmers was already elsewhere.

Chapter Twenty-Four

THE FRYING OF OTHER FISH

A development which spoils ten square miles of countryside will be the work of a few people neither particularly sinful nor malevolent. They may be called Derek or Malcolm, Hubert or Shigeru, they may love golf and animals and yet, in a few weeks, they can put in motion plans which will substantially ruin a landscape for 300 years or more.

Alain de Botton, *The Architecture of Happiness,* p.254.

On 21 October 1833, even as John Stallon stewed in the County Gaol in fear of his life, 'the proprietors of lands' in Great Shelford pulled up chairs in the *Eagle* public house in the centre of Cambridge for an inaugural meeting. [75]

Actually, this is a pre-meeting; the first *official* meeting will take place eight months from now, in June 1834. That meeting will last three days and will change the village of Great Shelford forever.

But let's stick with the pre-meeting. The purpose of the gathering is made crystal clear at the top of the minutes. '...*to consider of the propriety of inclosing the said Parish'.*[76]

The duty of chairing the meet is quickly given to Mr Samuel Prest, whose farm sits opposite the site where today the Baptist Chapel (or Free Church) stands in Great Shelford's High Street. Beneath the chair's name, thirteen more names are listed including those of both the Master and the Bursar of Jesus College, the Bursar of Gonville & Caius, and the Bursar of St John's College (all three colleges are major landowners in the village). It also includes the vicar of the parish, Rev. Henry Finch. The rest are farmers in the village, several of whom we might recognise. They include, in the order they appear in the list of those present – Peter Grain, Henry

Headly, William Headly and Thomas Stacey.

A letter from Edward Humphrys Green esquire – in support of the 'proposed measure' but regretting he cannot attend in person, is also acknowledged.

The meeting then adopts a number of resolutions: firstly, that application be made to the ensuing session of Parliament for an Act 'inclosing' the Parish and commuting the parish tithes. One twentieth of the Commons and Waste Lands are to be allotted in lieu of all Manorial rights of Soil within the parish. It is also agreed that one fifth of all the arable land and one eighth of the Meadows Pastures and other lands and ground will serve as compensation to the Impropriators of land for the commuted tithes. Impropriators include those who have received property as a benefice, ie the church and its vicar, and the colleges (whose roots are in religious houses).

With this principle settled, the meeting moves on to the granular business of how the above land, plus the remaining nineteen twentieths of the Commons, four fifths of arable lands, and seven eighths of the Meadow pastures belonging to the village will be divided between the claimants.

To those who have much will more be given is the general rule, but to achieve this tricky task fairly, the meeting appoints two Commissioners, one to be chosen by the proprietors, and one by the impropriators – together with an Umpire to settle disputes. The proprietors of lands have their commissioner already lined up, and the meeting resolves that Mr Edward Gibbons (of Northampton, gent) be appointed. The other will be named by the impropriators at their 'earliest convenience'. Both will later be named in the Act.

Mr George Cumming – a resident of the village – is appointed as the project's surveyor, and a legal firm, Pemberton & Hayward of Cambridge, (who have already been of service by placing the original ad in the 'paper) are appointed as solicitors.

There will later be some dispute over the choice of Commissioners, just as – much later, there will be barely contained outrage at the cost of Mr Cumming's work as surveyor.

As one of the bigger landowners in the village, Edward Green Esq. (he of the letter apologising for his absence to the first meeting) complains after this first meeting that he should have been afforded a say in the appointment of Commissioners, perhaps even nominating one himself. Too late. He was not present at the meeting.

The next set of minutes (another pre-meeting, dated Nov 21th, 1833) will reveal the second commissioner is now in place; Thomas Utton (of Brome in Suffolk, also gent) will represent the impropriators. Both the commissioners have previous experience of their role and are respectable people. In addition, as the solicitors patiently explain in a letter to the still-fuming Mr Green – the proprietors' man Edward Gibbons is an excellent choice since he is not only experienced in the role, but also lacks any links to the Cambridge Colleges. In the great carve up of land they are embarking on, the farmers are both in concert with, and in competition against, the ancient and powerful institutions that are the colleges. Their only hope is to ensure fair play.

As for Mr Cumming's bill, there is clear consternation at the end of the entire process over an invoice for his work as surveyor. Pemberton and Hayward (solicitors) are determined to push back: the bill from Cumming '...*not only very far exceeds the sum which...was set down in the minute...but...upon examination is very much beyond what the Commissioners conceive they would according to the Provision of the act of Parliament be justified in ordering.*' In response to the invoice of £850.7s, the Commissioners '*cannot make the bill exceed £650*'. Eventually – after the claim has been 'abated by his consent' – Mr Cumming settles for £728.9s.6d.[77]

George Cumming is not the only one to gain useful employment through the scheme. Hedges must be planted and fences must be built if the new parcels of land are to be clearly demarcated; tradesman must be appointed to carry out this work and legitimate expenses costed into the project.

In addition to all the above appointments, and in anticipation of disputes to come, a further, powerful committee is established in these early meetings. It comprises the Bursars of the three Colleges along with Edward Humphrys Green esquire (or his deputy), Samuel Prest and all the members of Shelford's Big Four. Its mission is to settle '*the Details of the Measure in conformity with the principles agreed above*'; to liaise with the trustees of Hobson's Conduit (a water supply by which the nearby city is provided for); and to '*make such arrangement as to them shall seem fit respecting the trees alleged to have been planted by the Poor on the Common and to be claimed by them.*'

The world 'alleged' is interesting here. It hints at the attituded towards the claims of those outside of the class of both proprietors and impropriators, who must nonetheless be dealt with under the scheme. Great Shelford is about to redraw the map of its territory, and the lives and rights of all those who work on it are affected – but none must resist the efficient execution of this quiet revolution – least of all, 'the Poor'.

Between now and the next meeting in June 1834 the Commissioners – Messrs Gibbons and Utton – will conduct a survey of 'proprietors of lands' in the village. Every farmer will be asked if they Assent to Enclosure, Dissent, or are Neutral on the subject. If the 'assenters' are in the majority, maps will be drawn up by Mr Cumming, and all the village's lands redistributed in as fair a way as possible. Any of the farmers may request their new-apportioned land is concentrated in a particular place (most want it close to home). Once the allocation is made, any farmer may lodge an objection, at which point the issue will be examined in detail by the committee just created for that purpose. If the committee cannot resolve the dispute, they have recourse to the Umpire, (a Mr Josselyn from Sproughton, Suffolk).[78]

The only people who may not complain – even though they stand to lose the most, at least in a theoretical sense – are the agricultural labourers who work the land, supplementing their income through their use of its Common and waste lands. They can make representations to the Committee about 'their' trees as we've seen, but regarding the key decision to Enclose the lands or not, they have no power. They are invited to none of the meetings above, much less asked to Assent or Dissent in the Commissioners' survey. Even if they can write, they are excluded from submitting their opinions.

What the agricultural workers lose in this process – in addition to whatever muted voice they formerly had – is a privilege they have enjoyed for many years, mainly by long-respected custom – providing they have 'Right of Commons'. This is a right tied to a house. It is stated as one of the benefits of the tenement John and Elizabeth lived in, when it was offered for sale. It is a right for the incumbents to use the village lands as their own. This includes the right to wander across it, but also the right to graze an animal or add an animal to the village herd; to collect wood or dig gravel or cut peat from the Commons – or to plant a fruit tree.

These rights, though maintained mainly by custom, were far from haphazardly policed. A document included with the Enclosure papers sets down 'Customs of stocking the Commons in the parish of Great Shelford' and tells us that 'the Shelford Commons are divided into several districts and are used by the persons entitled to Common Right…' These districts have age-old names; 'The High Green', 'The Baulks', 'The Back Moor', 'Crow Land' and 'May Pasture'. The right to use them is both extensive and highly regulated. Sheep owners, for example, are entitled to 'pastorage over and upon the above districts of common, over all the open lands and grounds, Commons, Commonable places and meadows within the whole parish from Old Christmas to Old Lady Day – except on the lands sewn with wheat, rye or turnips'.[79] [80]

In John Stallon's case, apart from the right to wander, these ancient rights were probably already reduced to theory. Owning a beast is beyond the means of most workers. This had become increasingly the case in recent years since prices for food had risen and risen while wages remain depressed. One estimate is that over a fifty-year period in the late 18th Century, prices rose in England by sixty percent, but wages by only twenty-five percent.[81] The idea of owning livestock is an ever-more distant dream, but that does not mean this change has no impact on the lives of people like John and Elizabeth Stallon.

What is being lost along with their Right of Commons is a possibility. Once a village is enclosed, all agricultural labourers will become entirely reliant on the wage paid by their employers. If work dries up – or it rains, or a worker gets sick and cannot work – they only have recourse to parish funds; they inevitably become paupers.

This prospect gives some farmers pause for thought. Others remain determined.

There is no doubt that the impulse towards greater productivity among the farmers of Great Shelford is genuine. As the journalist and historian Paul Johnson writes when discussing this agricultural revolution more generally:

Enclosure involved great cruelty and injustice…for it deprived great masses of the rural poor of marginal sources of food and income… [but] On the other hand…[it] undoubtedly prevented more misery than it caused, simply by allowing more food to be produced and marketed.[82]

This was important because the rising tide in England's population that had begun in the 18th Century was showing no sign of ebbing. Since 1780 the population had almost doubled, so that by 1831 it had risen from 7.1m to 13.1m.[83]

The Census in that year drove the message home. The poor – as Peter Grain would be keen to point out – do not feed themselves.

Such a moral/economic argument is compounded by a well-established view that the availability of a Right of Commons is actually *bad* for workers – and certainly for a society that needs their labour:

'...*moral effects of an injurious tendency accrue to the cottager, from a reliance on the imaginary benefits of stocking a common. The possession of a cow or two, with a hog, and a few geese, naturally exalts the peasant in his own conception...In sauntering after his cattle, he acquires a habit of indolence. Quarter, half, and occasionally whole days are imperceptibly lost. Day labour becomes disgusting; the aversion increases by indulgence; and at length the sale of a half-fed calf, or hog, furnishes the means of adding intemperance to idleness.*'

As another commentator adds, approvingly, Enclosure would thus be a great help in securing 'that subordination of the lower ranks of society which in the present times is so much wanting...'. [84]

For most farmers in 1833, the balance is between pursuing greater efficiency and profitability by rationalising the distribution of land – making it more amenable to 'modern' farming methods – versus safeguarding the livelihoods and prospects of labourers.

This choice inclines some farmers in Great Shelford to register themselves as Neutral in the Enclosure survey. In a very few cases, some even risk the fury and condemnation of their neighbours and list themselves as Dissenters. This in fact includes one of the bigger farmers in the village, Edward Humphrys Green, who having begun as a supporter of the scheme, finally turns up in the dissenting column. This may be out of pique following the earlier spat over the choice of Commissioner, or it may be the result of a genuine change of heart. Either way, Mr Green is in a minority.

In all, eighty-seven farmers are included in Great Shelford's survey – recorded under three headings, according to the amount of land they work; those who farm fewer than 10 acres; those whose land runs between eleven and fifty acres; and the ten farmers who hold more than fifty acres. Many small farmers are clearly sceptical about the cost-benefit ratio of the project: in this group, there is a very narrow majority in favour, if the neutrals are added to the dissenters – just twenty-three putting their mark in the assenting column, compared with twenty-two who do not. The balance however is firmly in favour in the two groups comprising the mid- and large-scale farmers. These farmers presumably calculate they have more to gain and little to lose from the change, and moreover see it as necessary progress. Overall, sixty-two farmers Assent, only ten Dissent. Even if the fifteen neutrals are added to the active dissenters, there is a clear majority for pressing forward.[85]

And press forward they do, for the men who attend these meeting at *The Eagle* are men in a hurry. As we've seen, the neighbouring village of Stapleford got all this sorted out fifteen years earlier.

Across South Cambridgeshire, the average length of time between an Act for Enclosure being moved in Parliament, and the Award being finalised by the commissioners, is six years. In Great Shelford, they will turn it around in twelve months. [86]

This suggests the farmers – or the Big Four on their behalf – have done their homework, squaring off most potential complaints or disputes ahead of the commissioners' work. They may be unfashionably late, but these are men who are more than ready to get the Enclosure party started.

At subsequent meetings, there are fewer people present. The project is underway; fields are being walked, maps are being drafted and contested allocations are being dealt with.

The show now runs itself.The five farmers who gather back at *The Eagle* to receive reports from the Commissioners in June 1834 are the village members of that extra committee, from which the college bursars seem to have absented themselves. The five who are present to receive reports are Samuel Prest in the chair, Peter Grain, Henry Headly, Thomas Stacey and William Headly.

Perhaps Shelford's Big Four just like their beer.

Chapter Twenty-Five

CONFESSIONS OF AN INCENDIARY

Confess your faults one to another, and pray one for another, that ye may be healed.

James, Chapter 5 v16.

First, denial.

Next, isolation.

From the bustle of the courtroom – so much noise, the fixed faces of his neighbours, and the terrible memory of Judge Littledale donning the black cap – John is returned to the County Gaol. There he is placed in a condemned cell to await enactment of his capital sentence.

Then a spark of hope; Mr Orridge informs John that he, as Governor, has received a respite order, for reasons that are as yet unclear.

It soon transpires the cause of the stay is a mere legal technicality - and that offers little for the prisoner to cling to. As the *Cambridge Independent Press* has it on 17th August, 1833:

...the fate of this convict is certain, whatever may be the decision with respect to the point of law, which at most could but give him the chances of a new trial in the first case, and protract his execution till the Spring Assizes...

In fact, a new date for execution is swiftly set. The hope that powered John's stirring pleas to the jury flickers, and gutters, and is gone.

To begin with, John responds to this blow by choosing silence.

There is defiance in this still, perhaps, and maybe some wisdom. For some time after he was first charged, John loudly protested his innocence. This enraged popular opinion, almost has much as his attempt to implicate his wife.

Of course, as a destroyer of property Stallon should expect no favours from the law or from the owners of the property destroyed (despite their insurance pay-outs). Some of the newspaper articles make this point explicitly. With no sense of irony, the *Bury and Norwich Post* fulminates on the subject:

> *The fact is, that he who has nothing like property of his own, will not hold very sacred the rights of property in others. This man Stallan is at this time under condemnation; a respite was sent down for him, in the expectation that further disclosures might be made, but it is not supposed that he will evade the extreme penalty of the law.* [87]

It is as though a person's lack of property is a result of personal inadequacy. Given that he has this moral weakness at his core, it is hardly surprising John should commit barbaric acts like arson.

Even if this reaction could have been anticipated, it is clear Stallon thinks he might have received some kinder treatment from his community. In John's worldview, it is the opinion of his community that most determines a man's identity. Immediately following the trial, the *Bury and Norwich Post* had reported the prisoner's rationale for staying silent: '...*as the parish and the world believe him to be guilty, and he is to suffer for it, it is unnecessary for him to say anything.*' [88]

Soon, however, John's stoic resolve begins to crumble. It is put to him by his new spiritual advisers at the prison that confession gifts the opportunity to make amends – in his case, for his implication of Elizabeth.

John himself might reason it this way: even if it were true that Elizabeth had a hand in setting or inspiring the fire at Mr Dean's, there is no point in the boys losing both parents. If he, John, confesses to setting all the fires he will bequeath to Elizabeth the status of a respectable, if gullible widow – a woman deserving of pity, if not quite respect. To bear the sins of others is an act more Christlike than any other...

On Tuesday the 20th of August, John confesses all. Some of his assertions – particularly those concerning Elizabeth are welcomed, as reported in the *Cambridge Chronicle* and syndicated in the newspapers of Leicester, Suffolk, Sligo, and elsewhere;

> *He says no other person was accessory to any of the fires, and he always most carefully and successfully concealed them from his wife, although on his first apprehension he had shamefully tried to exculpate himself by laying the guilt on her.*

Other details however, only fuel the condemnation vented by the press:

> *… John Stallan… was convicted of arson, at Cambridge, and confessed that, without being influenced by malice against the individuals, he had committed twelve different acts of incendiarism for the sake of the reward he got of six or seven shillings each time for playing the engines to extinguish the flames! The very flames that he had kindled with his own devilish torch. It is hardly possible to conceive such consummate ignorance and barbarism.*[89]

As previously noted, John made it very clear he had no hard feelings against his Master, Henry Headly, whose trust he abused. Both Henry, and his brother William, are good employers. When John is honest about the simple economic motive that was the chief driver of his actions, this inflames the newspapers still further. He did all this for a few shillings – *a paltry reward* – as the *Morning Post's* letter writer, 'A. Farmer' had put it.

Paltry for whom?

All the same, under guidance of Robert Orridge and the prison chaplains John has now made full confession, though he always strongly denies he had anything to do with the fire at Mr Stacey's. Thomas Stacey, as well as being a farmer, is also churchwarden of St Mary the Virgin. Maybe John shrank from torching the property of a fellow churchman – much less one, perhaps, who had shown him kindness on the frequent occasions

John and his family buried their relatives in his churchyard.

Confession made – and moral outrage vented – the newspapers are content to fit John Stallon into their required mould. He is portrayed in their further, frequent updates as the complete, quiescent criminal, repentant of his crimes, and accepting of the justice (and the rightness of that justice) that he has received so far – and will soon receive in full.

He (Stallon) made a full and unreserved confession to the Chaplain on Wednesday evening, and since then he says he has felt his mind much relieved.[90]

★

Elizabeth has been parked in the drawing room a full twenty minutes before the Reverend Finch appears. Uncertain whether to sit or stand, she has stood, her prayerbook clutched tightly to her chest – a talisman, one final straw – as if her back were not broken enough.

'I cannot write, Reverend', she says, once he creeps into view, 'You can. Other people will sign, if your name is seen first.'

Henry Finch shifts uneasily, but Elizabeth is still talking.

'For Thomas Cambridge it worked. And he wasn't to be killed, like John.'

'That is not comparable.'

''Ets a crime Reverend, I know that...'

'It was a fish!'

The Reverend immediately regrets raising his voice. Using his shoes for inspiration, he grinds out a reply.

'John is reconciled, Elizabeth. You must be too, for his sake'.

Elizabeth holds his gaze a painfully long time. At last she turns, then turns back – hurling the prayerbook at the great expanse of the drawing room window. The book smacks against the wooden sash and drops forlornly to the floor.

When the astonished vicar turns to face Elizabeth, she has vanished.

★

In late November, one week before his execution is due, Elizabeth and the children are allowed to visit John in prison.

We have no way of knowing what passes between the couple on this occasion. Elizabeth will later say about John – the same man called a 'devil' and a 'fiend', and to whom was attributed 'pure diabolical motives' – that 'a more affectionate husband or tender father never existed'.[91]

Despite John turning the finger of accusation towards her, imperilling her with the same dreadful fate he is now facing, Elizabeth it seems, bears him no ill-will.

I imagine John giving his tiny wife a matching, crooked smile when she visits; 'People did always underestimate you, Elizabeth'.

Or perhaps it is poor John Junior who receives John's most important words. This is a nine-year-old, finding himself inside the County Gaol, the most terrifying place on earth, sensing things are only going to get worse. He has been told by the village boys, if not by his mother, that his father will be hanged before Christmas. And it could be all his fault.

'Don't follow me in this, John', says his father, 'Practice your letters...' and perhaps he adds a brief word of warning; '...and do not play with matches'.

Little William of course is a mere twenty months old. As long as he has been alive, his father has been scorching the earth – earth that William has now begun to walk upon. Personally, I hope toddler William later remembers none of this visit to the prison, except perhaps that his father was tender with him, and that his mother held him tightly.

And then the visit is over. It is time for Elizabeth and John Jr and William to exit through one door of the prison while John awaits his own exit, through another.

Chapter Twenty-Six

A WEIRD KIND OF HOLIDAY

The culprit Stallan, whose execution will take place to-morrow at 12 o'clock, expresses himself perfectly resigned to his awful fate, and pays uniform attention to the spiritual help afforded to him.
Cambridge Chronicle & Journal, 6 December, 1833.

The morning of 7 December, 1833 was an overcast and blustery one. It may be a cliché to say, 'the condemned man ate a hearty breakfast', but when the *Suffolk Chronicle* catches up with events two weeks later, it assures us that John Stallon had eaten heartily the night before his ordeal, and that he enjoyed a good night's sleep. On the morning itself, he was offered communion and then set off on the customary trip around the prison, taking leave of his fellow prisoners. He advised them to learn from his mistakes, and to change their ways.[92]

As he did these rounds, John would no doubt be conscious of a stirring outside the prison, for quite some jamboree is gathering pace. In a report given by the *Essex Herald,* it's clear the citizens of Great Shelford are out in force, along with many, many, others. The report also makes clear which aspect of Stallon's crimes the newspaper finds most abhorrent. It is equally clear that whatever the poet John Donne might believe, John is very much an island. It being Saturday, most males of John's class – or at least those lucky enough to be employed – are in the fields:

There were present about 10,000 persons, (a great proportion of them females) who came from the neighbouring villages, and more

especially from Shelford – the scene of his crimes… The property which
he had been the means of destroying is calculated at £60,000… The
spectators before the gaol behaved with great decorum: but no pity was
expressed for the fate of the criminal…[93]

John Stallon, arsonist, had long provided fuel for newspapers;
next day, he is the sole subject of a bulletin or 'broadside'
distributed on the streets of Cambridge:

Two sections of this broadside rehearse the details of John's
life and his crimes, followed by a summary of the trial and
his subsequent confession. These sections plainly reproduce
copy drawn from newspaper coverage from the last two years.
Then a third section describes the execution itself in direct,
and typically judgemental terms:

A few minutes before 12 o'clock the wretched culprit approached
the fatal platform, accompanied by the Rev. Mr Ventris, the chaplain,
and Mr. Orridge, the governor of the prison, when after a few minutes
spent in reading that portion of the burial service used on such
occasions, in which the unhappy criminal appeared fervently to join,
the executioner having adjusted the cord, and the bolt withdrawn,
the victim of lawless outrage, in view of an immense assemblage
of spectators, made his exit from a world he had offended by the
perpetration of one of the most horrid crimes that disgraces our nature.

There follows a ballad, written in the first person, relating
the tale of John's life and crimes in nine short stanzas. This is

obviously composed by someone else – or is it? Is it possible
that John Stallon, ballad writer, would get the name of his final
victim wrong? Could he have called William Dean, Richard
by mistake? Of course not. It is just another close brush with
the genuine voice of The Firestarter – and one twisted to the
values of the status quo he had shaken but which had finally
destroyed him. It is still worth a listen:

Good people hearken unto one
Whose wicked course is nearly run,
While I my awful crimes relate,
Which brings me to this dreadful fate.

A few years since I little thought,
I to the scaffold should be brought;
And held up there to public scorn,
For burning of my neighbour's corn.

At Shelford was this sad affair,
Led on by wicked motives there,
I took the most unlawful means,
To burn the barn of Richard Deans.

My precious soul is I know at stake,
Confession therefore I do make;
To serve a wicked selfish turn,
Twelve times I made the fires to burn.

For which I've been condemned to die,
And end my days in misery;
O grant it may a warning prove,
And hardened sinners tend to move.

What will my wife and children think
To see me on destruction's brink,

O'erwhelmed with grief, despair, and woe
At seeing my sad overthrough.

Young men think on my warning voice,
And hearken to my last advice;
Let not your passions have full vent,
Or you'll have reason to repent.

Before I've scarcely passed my prime,
I'm cut off for this wicked crime,
For setting of the stacks in flame,
I end my days in dread and shame.

A few short hours is all allow'd
Before I meet the dreadful crowd;
When justice ends her destiny,
And views me in eternity! [94]

Rather surprisingly to those of us who believed that an executed criminal could not be buried in consecrated ground, the final detail of the *Cambridge Chronicle* account of the execution is telling:

Shortly after one o'clock the body was removed from the castle in a tilted cart to Shelford, the village in which the culprit had long lived, and where he has occasioned so much alarm and destruction…

The career, and life, of the Shelford Arsonist was over. And now he was going home.

BOOK FIVE

HORKEY

Chapter Twenty-Seven

EXORCISM, AND AFTER

All evils are to be considered with the good that is in them…
Daniel Defoe, *Robinson Crusoe.*

In the seasonal calendar common to rural communities in Britain at the start of the nineteenth century, the festival of Harvest Home was a high point.

In fact, 'Horkey' – as it was known in Cambridgeshire – was only one of three key feasts associated with the season of harvest, beginning with a 'taking supper'.

Agricultural labourers announced their availability for harvest by scraping their reaping hooks on the hardened surface of a farmer's yard. Then negotiations began. At stake was the price to be paid to each man for bringing in the harvest, and this negotiation was quite a business. Fields were inspected by the workers' chosen leader in the company of the farmer; a rate was offered by the farmer, rejected by the labourers, and a counter offer eventually accepted. The hours worked during harvest would be long, but wages could be double what was paid in other months. This was the season when workers could clear their debts, and hopefully put something by, so the fixing of the rate was key to their survival for the rest of the year. Not surprisingly, the triumphant chief negotiator was declared 'Lord of the Harvest'. The Taking Supper followed; a meal supposedly fortifying the workers for the labour ahead – or maybe, just beer was distributed, and a shilling on top of the agreed wage added as a token of goodwill.

A 'Half-way Supper' marked the midpoint of the crop-gathering, and then, finally, it was time for the 'Harvest

Home'. When the last sheaves had been carted and stacked, this climactic blow-out was preceded by the loading of the Horkey Cart, driven by the Lord of the Harvest, accompanied by a pretty young woman as his Queen.

Paraded through the village in late September, the Horkey Cart was greeted with loud shouts and singing.

There was a mystic side to Harvest Home too. From the last sheaf of corn, representing the spirits of the field, straw was tightly plaited to make a harvest doll. This was then soaked with water, or beer, to ensure good rains the following spring.

And then the partying began. [95]

As the *Encyclopaedia Brittanica* suggests, Harvest Home had pagan roots albeit with a Christian gloss:

> *'The ancient festival also included the symbolic murder of the grain spirit, as well as rites for expelling the devil'.*[96]

Clearly, Horkey came late to Great Shelford in 1833. Their current devil – John Stallon – had been expelled in the most comprehensive way possible, just weeks before Christmas.

All the same, the village was not exactly celebrating. In fact, it was about to do for John Stallon (deceased), what it could not – or would not – do for John while he was alive.

John's body was taken from the County Gaol and brought to the bosom of his parish in a tilted cart.

As ever, I am intrigued by the nuts and bolts of this. The bulletin's account is clear that a tilted cart was used to take the body to burial. But whose tilted cart was it? Who was it who sat behind the ample behind of a horse and drove the cart, the horse's hooves clacking out their sad toll all the way to John's last resting place? The graveyard was the same place that John had buried his daughter and brother, that of St Mary the Virgin in the heart of Great Shelford. It would have been quite a journey.

Perhaps it was the prison's own horse and cart that was used,

Robert Orridge giving permission for its loan to the family. Or perhaps it belonged to John's erstwhile master Henry Headly, that 'best of masters' who seems of all the principals to have kept the lowest profile during the trial. Did he now feel he could, at last, respond kindly for the sake of John's widow?

Personally, I like to think William Cambridge, or even Thomas Willers might take some responsibility and make a cart available. They had the means and were such close neighbours. John's son had run around their yards probably, and greeted them politely.

The cart supplier might even have been Peter Grain, in his role as quasi village mayor.

Once at the church, the Reverend Henry Finch officiates.

A service can't be avoided, obviously. As noted at the beginning of this account, in the Appendix to the published sermon preached by Rev. Edward Baines MA, Fellow of Christ's College, the theme is explicitly political. Rev Baines condemns what in modern terminology he would call the 'dependency culture' – which in his eyes is created by the parish poor relief system. This, he says, is responsible for the *monstrous and still increasing mischief* that is incendiarism:

Till this eating-canker is healed, the high and manly spirit of self-supporting independence, which once graced and upheld the character of the English peasant, will continue to sicken and languish, and be less and less seen each returning harvest.[97]

In the sermon itself, point-scoring of a spiritual nature was the Reverend's objective, decrying the 'atrocious wickedness' which had brought John Stallon to his 'merited end':

...the defiled and the abominable, the haters of God and the despiser of God, those that love sin and those that have no love for righteousness, shall be cast into the outer darkness, where there shall be 'weeping, and wailing, and gnashing of teeth'.

Is he really talking about John Stallon? *Our* John Stallon? The one who never hurt, much less killed, anyone?

I hope Elizabeth, and especially John Jr were spared this unremitting castigation of the man they had lost, the firestarter they loved. No child needs to hear their beloved parent is lost to eternal damnation, however deserving of it some might think they are.

Soon enough, thank God, the service is over. And then the burial.

★

In the freezing cold vestry, separated from Bob Doel and myself only by that crucial couple of centuries, the Rev Finch – the same Rev Henry Finch who had baptised John and Elizabeth as babes, and then joined their hands in marriage – now enters John Stallon's name in the burial register, in a beautiful flowing hand.

Perhaps Henry is nervous, for while the hand is good, the Rev makes a mess of the layout. All the extra information he feels obliged to include needs to be squashed into the unyielding rows and columns of the register. Unravelled, it reads like this:

John Stallan – called Stallion – executed for Arson at the County Gaol in Cambridge, interred in the parish of Great Shelford December 8 1833 aged 33 years.

In the column labelled 'officiating minister', Henry Finch signs his name.

I click the camera on my phone, and Bob shows me back into the slightly less-glacial main body of the church. I pass to my left the chancel arch and turn to see the doom painting – sheep to the right, goats to the left – all the order of the Final Judgement, restored.

Still, at least John is back in Great Shelford, even if it is in the graveyard. Now there is just the fate of the living for us to worry about, beginning with John's widow – a woman they often referred to at the time as his 'relict' – his wife, Elizabeth.

★

The name Stallon is mercifully absent from the newspapers in the immediate aftermath of John's funeral. The name of Shelford does crop up, however; the village, as we've seen, is preoccupied with the complicated business of Enclosure.

Luckily for us, the 1841 census for Great Shelford does survive (unlike the 1831 version), and this is a good indication of who lived where. Were Elizabeth and her children also welcomed back into the village?

At first, a search entered into the digital copy of the survey fails to find any mention of Elizabeth Stallon, Stallan, Stallion or Stallen living in the village. Only when I trawl through the census page by page, street by street, do I find her. By dint of the barely legible writing of the recorder, she is hiding away on page six, ducking the attention of the search engine.

Elizabeth has moved out of the tenement owned by Thomas Willers. She is now living in College Cottages, a few minutes' walk from Woollards Lane, towards High Green. In fact, these may be the cottages referred to in *Domesday to Dormitory: A History of the Landscape of Great Shelford*:

Another kind of building development which started in the early 19th century, and which was to become very important later on was the erection of buildings on High Green. This ancient meadow and common land had remained empty of buildings throughout the medieval period and later but with the continued demand for more houses buildings now started being erected on the Green. A group of five or six cottages was built on the open High Green…though they have long since been demolished. [98]

This short-lived row of cottages may have been built by the parish for its poorest inhabitants – ironically, on former common land. In the census column labelled 'occupation', there is some very faint writing beside Elizabeth's name. I think I can make out the word '*Pauper*' – meaning that Elizabeth is indeed supported by the parish. Living with her is her younger son William, aged nine.

I find Elizabeth's older son, John Junior, living very close by, in the residence of Mr George Twiss, attorney, in Great Shelford's High Street.

It may seem ironic (again) that John, whose father was executed just a few years earlier, is now being sheltered by the County Coroner who in all likelihood was the man responsible for inspecting John Sr's body and pronouncing him dead after his execution. I prefer to see an act of kindness in this. Imagine Elizabeth's relief at having one fewer mouth to feed, scraping by as she is on parish handouts. Knowing that John Stallon Jr. is, at the age of seventeen (stated as fifteen in the census) living in a respectable household, and no doubt being encouraged to develop his literacy skills – all this would likewise be a source of pride to Elizabeth, or at least gratitude.

Ten years later, in the census of 1851, John is still living with Mr Twiss and his wife Bertha, though his employers now have two children of their own, and John has the title of General House Servant. In this role he works alongside a Housekeeper & Cook of a similar age, named Elizabeth Whybrow. My own maternal grandparents, Harry Williams and Nita Johnson, met in the exact same way. The impression is of a young man keeping his head down and perhaps making plans, well away from the cruel fields and uncertainties of the agricultural labourer's life.

By this time, Elizabeth herself has passed away. In 1848, aged fifty-five, she in her turn is swallowed by the parish burial register. She has joined John, and the first of their children Ann, and also (we believe) John's brutally slain brother William, in the graveyard of St Mary the Virgin. Like the rest of her family, Elizabeth has no stone to mark the spot where her body —so small and 'rather deformed' and worn by care — is buried.

William Stallon the younger meanwhile, has disappeared from Great Shelford completely.

Chapter Twenty-Eight

THE ONE WHO GOT AWAY

The Phantasmascope. This is a new and exceedingly ingenious toy, designed by Professor Plateau, of Brussels, and first introduced to England at the meeting of the British Association at Cambridge. It consists of a series of cards, which being revolved before a looking glass, reflect the figures of animals in motion with such truth as to excite not merely astonishment, but admiration.
Hereford Journal Weds 14 August 1833

Tracking the movements of young William Stallon after the death of his mother is difficult. It is only made possible by the familial loyalty of his parents.

William's middle name – taken from Elizabeth's side of the family – is 'Patman'.

The name also produces more mystery.

Not until 1871, by which time William is thirty-nine years old, do I find a William Stallan (sic) counted in the census. He is living in Cambridge, in the parish of St Andrews. He has married a woman from Suffolk, Matilda, and they have three children aged six years, five years, and five months respectively, and he gives his place of birth as 'Cambs, Shelford'. His living is made as a 'fly proprietor' – a cab driver – and the family live at Number 28, Jesus Lane.

Is it really *our* William who is kept awake by the baby at night? His eldest child is called Ann Elizabeth, which is perhaps a clue; they are the names of William's grandmother, Ann Fen, and his mother – though it's true they are common enough names.

For conclusive evidence we have to wait until the 1891 census, when the family turn up in the nearby parish of St Botolph's. Now there are more children, all crammed into an address in Black Lion Yard in Silver Street. Ann Elizabeth and her little brother Harry – who was her youngest brother in 1871, at five months – are no longer living with their parents. Whether there is tragedy or simple progression behind that, we have no way of knowing. Twenty-five year-old William Thomas however is still at home and working as printer; his brother Joseph, 18, is a porter (presumably at one of the colleges); their sister Alice, seventeen, is a domestic servant, and Georgina, aged thirteen years, is listed as a 'scholar'. There is one more member of the household, a toddler named William Rose aged two years, listed as 'grandson'.

As for Grandfather William, he has stayed in the trade in which he began; he is now listed as 'Fly driver, Groom'. He is fifty-seven. Crucially, he still gives his birthplace as Shelford in Cambridgeshire, but now bravely adds the initial of his middle name: 'P'.

What happened to William Patman Stallon when he first left Great Shelford? I check out military records, without success. On a hunch, I search for William Patman in the 1851 census, and find one such, aged nineteen (the age of our William at that time), living in St Botolph's parish in what seems to be a boarding house run by a Mr and Mrs Purser. The boarding house is in Black Lion Yard, Silver Street – the very place William is later found living with his enlarged family.

In 1851 William was listed as a lodger, though giving his birthplace as Bradly in Suffolk. Was William's instinct – like that of his brother John – to keep a low profile after his father's death?

In March 1850, the *Cambridge Chronicle* was still rerunning the story of the Shelford Firestarter, who lit twelve fires for the pay he got for putting them out. John Stallon Sr is referred to in the article as 'the last man to have been executed in Cambridge' – by which, sadly, it can only mean 'the last to be executed for arson'. Seven years later it was no longer a capital crime. A young man, trying to make a fresh start, might well decide to play down his connection to that traumatic story.

Whatever the truth of that, William has succeeded in establishing some level of respectability – and stability – in his case, as a cab driver.

This has come at a price, though William might not count it so. His wing of the Stallon family is no longer made up of agricultural labourers; they are estranged from the land. William is however giving shelter to the vulnerable in the form of little William Rose.

He is also earning a steady living, working with animals. I think his father would be proud of that.

Epilogue I

In London, aged 76, Mr Robert Orridge, late governor of the county gaol, Cambridge, accidentally killed by a wagon passing over him.

The Gentleman Magazine, Vol XLV, May, 1856.

Epilogue II

She is early in the yard behind her pauper's cottage. Relict or not, washing has to be done – her own washing, and other people's washing too. Rinsed of stains, made grimeless, she scrubs the hems of shirts and smocks and wrings them till her hands are red-raw. Then she is battling with the line and prop, as she has battled all her life.

When the washing is finally aloft, she wipes her hands on her apron, tosses a glance at the world just visible above the wall of the little yard, and retreats indoors.

Outside, playing against the sky in a blustery wind, the blouses and smocks, shirts and trousers of the busy people of Shelford fill with air.

They twist and buck, like a foretaste of a summer fair.

ACKNOWLEDGEMENTS

Anyone who writes history – even of the speculative kind – stands on the shoulders of giants.

A much-thumbed copy of the *Great Shelford Chronicle* held by Shelford Library first set me on the trail of John Stallon – alongside Helen Harwood's local history website.

Shirley Wittering, author of a peerless study of *Enclosure in South Cambridgeshire,* provided me with lots of context. Both authors were kind enough to answer queries by email when I got stuck.

To date, I haven't met either of these impressive detectives in person; I hope I will now.

Fanny Wale I sadly can't meet, but her curiosity about The Shelford Arsonist preceded mine by a hundred years. As the current book reveals, her notes and maps were vital in unravelling certain mysteries.

Staff at the National Archives at Kew, Cambridgeshire Archives in Ely, the Cambridge Collection at the Central Library, and Cambridge University Library, were also generous with their time, and on occasion, eyesight. I'd also like to thank Iain Stewart and his staff at Wimpole Hall for allowing me access to hidden areas of the house, and for answering many questions.

My dearest writing friends, Andrea Porter and Miranda Doyle both read drafts or excerpts and offered helpful suggestions, as did regular readers Jan Connor and Ciaran Grace. The errors that remain are all my own work.

Lewis Grace fed us during lockdown and as always, kept our spirits up.

Robert and Sophia at Galileo Publications have a been a great encouragement. Their enthusiasm for my telling of the story, and the care they've taken in bringing our book into being has been a great gift.

Finally, thanks to my wife Sue, without whom… There are no words.

ENDNOTES

1   Alan Bulwinkle, ed., *The Great Shelford Chronicle*, (Cambridge: Great Shelford Parish Council, 1993), p.22.

2   Aaron O'Neill, *Child mortality in the United Kingdom 1800-2020*, <https://www.statista.com/statistics/1041714/united-kingdom-all-time- child-mortality-rate/> [accessed, 9 September 2024]

3   Enid Porter, *Cambridgeshire Customs and Folklore*, (London: Routledge and Kegan Paul, 1969), pp.187, 272.

4   Enid Porter, *Cambridgeshire Customs and Folklore*, (London: Routledge and Kegan Paul, 1969), pp.187, 272.

5   E.J. Hobsbawm and George Rudé, *Captain Swing*, (London: Penguin University Books, 1969), p.224.

6   Handbill reporting 'a meeting of the magistrates at Cambridge, this 3rd day of December 1830', reproduced in David Ellison, *Captain Swing Stilled in Our Corner of Cambridgeshire by Philip Yorke, 3rd Earl of Hardwicke,* undated Mock-up Copy, held in Cambridgeshire Collection, C.44.17Reference Reserve.

7   Ellison, (undated), pp.7-9.

8   Judge Baron Vaughan, sentencing Reader, Turner & Howard, *Huntingdon, Bedford & Peterborough* Gazette, Saturday 20 March, 1830.

9   *Cambridge Chronicle and Journal* - Friday 16 December, 1831.

10   Agronomic Crops Network, University of Ohio, *Hay and Straw Barn Fires a Real Danger,* <https://agcrops.osu.edu/newsletter/corn-newsletter/2017-19/hay-and-straw-barn-fires-real-danger > [accessed 27 September 2024]

11   *Cambridge Chronicle and Journal* - Friday 20 April, 1827.

12   Fanny Lucretia Wale, *A Record of Shelford Parva*, (Cambridge: Little Shelford Local History Society and Little Shelford Parish Council, 2012).
The book is being republished in 2025 by Galileo Publishers.

13   Automated machines for mass producing clay roof tiles were first patented in the 1870s. By the 1880s a lot more factories were starting to make use of the new machines.
Heritage Clay Tiles Ltd, *The History of Clay Tiles* < https://heritagetiles.co.uk/index.php?p=articles-the-history-of-clay-roof-tiles >[accessed 25 May 2022].

14   Oliver Rackham, *The History of the Countryside,* (London: Weidenfield & Nicolson, 2020), p.190.

15   John Denson of Waterbeach, *A Peasant's Voice to Landowners*, 1830, reprinted, (Cambridge: Cambridgeshire Records Society, 1991). pp. xx-xxi.

16   *Bury and Norwich Post* - Wednesday 8 March, 1820.

17   Merryn & Raymond Williams, *John Clare: Selected Poetry and Prose*, (London: Methuen English Texts, 1986), p.10.

18   Ibid., pp.147-150.

19   Ibid., p.90.

20   Ibid., p.93.

21   John Clare, letter to John Taylor, 5 Feb 1822, in Mark Storey, ed., *John Clare: Selected Letters* (Oxford: Oxford University Press, 1988), p.67.

22   John Clare, *The Old Man's Lament,* < https://www.simple-poetry.com/poems/the-old-man-s-lament-53262350984> [accessed 4 October 2024]

23   Clare, letter to Marianne Marsh early January 1832, in Storey, 1988, p.176.

24   Clare's poem *Rememberances* is the exception, written in 1832, though this too remained unpublished until 1908. Other poems that mention Enclosure – e.g. *The Mores,* and *The Lament of Swordy Well* – were written in the early part of the 1820s but only published in 1935 – more than sixty years after Clare's death in 1864. See Williams, (1968).

25   Clare, letter to Marianne Marsh July 6, 1831, in Storey, 1988, p.171.

26   Withers, quoted by Enid Porter, *A Village Poet,* Cambridgeshire Life, March 1970, p.46-7.

27   James Reynolds Withers, *Poems upon Various Subjects,* Second Edition, (Cambridge: CW Naylor 1856) pp137-139.< https://www.wildhead.co.uk/_files/ ugd/17d082_1ccd5d12ab53489790c04d964c5f142d.pdf> [accessed 20 June 2022]

28   The National Archives, Kew – Home Office, (HO) 64/2/116.

29   *Cambridge Chronicle and Journal* – Friday 30 December, 1831.

30   HO 17/32/33.

31   Original MS of Wedd's elevation, in DE/B1737 – *title deed and misc personal and business papers*, Hertfordshire Archive & Local Studies, County Hall, Hertford.

32   Alfred Kingston, *Fragments of Two Centuries: Glimpses of Country Life When George III was King* first pubd. Royston: Warren Brothers 1893, via Project Gutenberg, <https://www.gutenberg. org/files/21352/21352-h/21352-h.htm#chap14 > [accessed 9 September 2024].See also, Enid Porter, Cambridge Stage Coaches, *Cambridgeshire, Peterborough and Huntingdon Life,* April, (1968). pp19-21.

and:
Peter Speak, and Shirley Whittering (eds.), Thriplow Journal Vol. 13/3 Spring (2005). <https://www.thriplow.org.uk/thriplow-society/wp-content/uploads/2017/01/2004-vol-13.3.pdf>[accessed 10 September 2024].

33   < https://capturingcambridge.org/centre/green-street/24-green-street/ >[accessed 11 September 24]

34   For more on the composition, functioning, and governance of the Principal Officers in general, see David J. Cox, *A Certain Share of Low Cunning: A history of the Bow Street Runners, 1792-1839,* (London: Routledge, 2012).

35   Ibid., p.172.

36   PF Hetherington, *Chronicles of the Bow Street Police-Office,* (London: Chapman & Hall, 1888), p.92.

37   *Bury and Norwich Post* – Wednesday 12 April, 1820.

38   Letter quoted in Cox, (2012), p.124.

39   The *Globe* - Friday 06 January, 1832.

40   Ibid.

41   Exeter University, < https://evidencebasedjustice.exeter.ac.uk/case/stefan-kiszko/>
[accessed, 20 May 2022].

42   The Guardian, < https://www.theguardian.com/law/2024/sep/11/the-dice-is-loaded-the-fight-to-clear-oliver-campbells-name-after-34-years?> [accessed 20/09/24] BBC News, <https://www.bbc.co.uk/news/articles/c70j2d4v24wo > [accessed 20 September 24]

43   Cox, (2012), note 79, p63.

44   For these and other details of the case see transcript by William Brodie Gurney, *The Trials of Arthur Thistlewood, John Thomas*

Brunt, Richard Tidd, William Davidson and others for High Treason, Vol II (1820), republished USA: Scholar Select, undated.

45   Ibid., pp.184-5.

46   Ibid., pp.190-91.

47   Father Frank Ryan, (undated), *The wrongful conviction & execution of James Pratt & John Smith for 'buggery' in 1835,* <https://www.petertatchellfoundation.org/pratt-smith-last-uk-men-hanged-for-sodomy > [accessed 20 May 2022]

48   Quoted by David R Bentley, (1993), *Trial on Indictment in Nineteenth Century England,* unpublished Doctoral Thesis, Sheffield University Faculty of Law, citing 46.

49   National Archive, Kew - ASSI 32/28, Crown Minute Book, 1831-34, Lent.

50   Taunton is believed to be the anonymous author of '*A Reminiscence of a Bow Street Officer*', published in *Harper's New Monthly Magazine* in September 1852. see Cox, (2012), p.245.

51   The Weekly Dispatch - March 17, 1822, p.83.

52   Arthur Rook, Margaret Carlton and W. Graham Cannon, *The History of Addenbrooke's Hospital Cambridge,* (Cambridge University Press, 1991), p49. This references Addenbrooke's Hospital Minute Book, Weekly Meeting, 19/1/1767, and an entry in Minutes of the Governors of Addenbrooke's Hospital: Volume 1 (Catalogue: AHGR 3/1/1/1).

53   Elizabeth Hurren and Steve King, *Begging for a Burial: Form, Function and Conflict in Nineteenth Century Pauper Burial,* Social History, Vol 30, No. 3, August 2005, pp.321-341, [accessed via JStor, 26 February 2022].

54   *Leicester Journal* - Friday 23 August, 1833.

55   George Boase & William Prideaux Courtney, *Bibliotheca*

Cornubiensis, Vol.2, (Cornwall: Longmans, Green, Reader and Dyer, 1850), p.439.

56   HO 64/3, p.295-6.

57   HO 64/3, p.299.

58   HO 64/3, p.297.

59   The Bury and Norwich Post - Friday 6 April, 1832.

60   Morning Post - Thursday 25 April, 1833.

61   *Huntingdon, Bedford and Peterborough Gazette* - Saturday 4 May, 1833.

62   Cambridge University Library (CUL), House of Commons Parliamentary Papers, 1834 XXXIV, *The Royal Commission into the Operation of the Poor Laws,* Appendix A, p.592a, and 1834 44 vol XXX, Appendix B(1)1, p.64a.

63   National Archive, Kew - T 38/674 : Treasurers Departmental Accounts, Receiver's Accounts Public Office, Bow Street.

64   *Cambridge Chronicle & Journal* - Friday 3 February, 1832.

65   *Cambridge Chronicle & Journal* - Trial Report, Friday 2 August, 1833.

66   John E. Archer, *By A Flash And A Scare: Arson, Animal Maiming and Poaching in East Anglia 1815-1870,* (London: Breviary Stuff, 2020), p.24, p.70.

67   Cambridge Castle, < https://capturingcambridge.org/ museum-of-cambridge/museum-exhibit-stories/cambridge-castle > [accessed 29 March 2022] see also, James Neild, *An Account of the Rise, Progress And Present State of the Society for the Discharge and Relief of Persons Imprisoned for Small Debts Throughout England and Wales,* (London: John Nichols & Son, 1808), pp.124-126. <https:// www.google.co.uk/books/edition/An_Account_of_the_Rise_Prog-

ress_and_Pres/4RMwAAAAYAAJ?hl=en&gbpv=1&dq=robert+or-ridge+cambridge+county+gaol&pg=PA124&printsec=frontcover[-accessed> [accessed 29 September 2024].

68   *Cambridge Chronicle and Journal* - Friday 3 June, 1836.

69   Ibid., Saturday 10 January, Thursday 15 January, 1846.

70   John Simpkin, *Average Child Height in 1836,* Spartacus Educational, September 1997, updated, January 2020 < https://spartacus-educational.com/IRheight.htm >[accessed 20 September 2022].

71   An example of the ritual in Cambridge is described in the *Bury and Norwich Post,* Wednesday 4 August, 1830.

72   *Cambridge Chronicle and Journal* - Friday 2 August, 1833.

73   HO 17/32/35

74   HO 17/31/138

75   CUL Doc 652 - Great Shelford Enclosure Papers, Minutes of Meeting, October 21, 1833. I'm indebted to Shirley Wittering, for directing me to the original documents, and for her careful analysis of the process(es) of Enclosure throughout South Cambridgeshire. See Shirley Wittering, *Ecology and Enclosure: The Effect on Society, Farming and the Environment in South Cambridgeshire, 1798-1850,* (Oxford: Windgather Press, 2013), pp.65-82.

76   CUL Doc 652(3), Copy of Resolutions of Meeting 21 October, 1833.

77   CUL 652, Letter from Pemberton & Hayward, 16 December, 1835.

78   Cambridgeshire Archives, Ely - *Act for Inclosing Lands in the Parish of Great Shelford in the County of Cambridge, and for commuting tithes of the said Parish,* Great Shelford Inclosure Minute Book, p.4. K 107/O/C/7, Commissioners' Papers, K107/O/C/28.

79   CUL DOC 652/113, CUL DOC 652, GBR/0012/MS
Doc.

80   In 1752, the British Empire switched from the Julian
Calendar to the Gregorian Calendar, putting itself in line with most
of western Europe. This set back the traditional start of the annual
business cycle by eleven days. Rather than contracts being dated
and rents etc being due on Lady Day (March 25) they were now
anchored to the 5 April - called, confusingly, Old Lady Day. Old
Christmas Day is January 6.

81   Nathan Zipfel, *Agriculture & the Labourer*,< https://www.
engcam.org/index.php/history-articles/84-agriculture-the-labourer
> (EnglandGenWeb Project, 2014), [accessed, 8 March 2022].

82   Paul Johnson, *A History of the English People,* Revised
Edition, (London: Weidenfeld Paperbacks, 1985), pp. 269-70.

83   Christopher Harvey and H.C.G. Matthew, *Nineteenth
Century Britain: A Very Short Introduction,* (Oxford University Press,
2000), p.11.

84   These views from just before the turn of the nineteenth
century, quoted by Hammond, JL and Barbara Hammond, *The Village
Labourer 1760-1832,* (London: Longmans, Green, and Co., 1911),
pp.37-38.

85   Wittering,(2013), p.70.

86   Ibid., p.72.

87   Bury & Norwich Post - Wednesday 9 October, 1833.

88   Ibid., Wednesday 14 August, 1833.

89   Ibid., Wednesday, 9 October, 1833.

90   *Leicester Journal* - Friday 23 August, 1833.

91   *Cambridge Independent Press* – Saturday 14 December, 1833.

92   *The Suffolk Chronicle or Weekly General Advertiser & County Express* – Saturday 14 December, 1833.

93   *Essex Herald* – Tuesday 10 December, 1833.

94   Broadside: *Life, Trial, Confession and Execution of John Stallan, who was executed at Cambridge, December 7th, for arson.* <https://id.lib.harvard.edu/curiosity/crime-broadsides/46-990031890620203941> [accessed Friday 27 May, 2022]

95   Porter, (1969), p.120.

96   *Encyclopaedia Brittanica*, < https://www.britannica.com/topic/Harvest-Home> [accessed March 01, 2022].

97   Revd. Edward Baines MA, *Funeral Sermon on John Stallan, Who Was Executed for Arson,* (Cambridge: printed at the Pitt Press by John Smith, printer to the University, 1833), Appendix.

98   CC Taylor (ed.), *Doomsday to Dormitory: The History of the Landscape of Great Shelford,* (Cambridge Local History Group, 1970), p.29.